WITHDRAWN
HARVARD LIBRARY
WITHDRAWN

Missionary Rivalry and Educational Expansion in Nigeria, 1885-1945

Missionary Rivalry and Educational Expansion in Nigeria, 1885-1945

Magnus O. Bassey

Studies in the History of Missions
Volume 15

The Edwin Mellen Press
Lewiston•Queenston•Lampeter

Library of Congress Cataloging-in-Publication Data

Bassey, Magnus O.
  Missionary rivalry and educational expansion in Nigeria, 1885-1945 / Magnus O. Bassey.
    p.   cm. -- (Studies in the history of missions ; v. 15)
  Includes bibliographical references and index.
  ISBN 0-7734-8153-2 (hard)
  1. Education and state--Nigeria--History. 2. Missions--Educational work--Nigeria--History. 3. Educational change--Nigeria--History. I. Title. II. Series.
  LC95.N55B37   1999
  379.669--dc21   99-12629
                                                                         CIP

This is volume 15 in the continuing series
Studies in the History of Missions
Volume 15 ISBN 0-7734-8153-2
SHM Series ISBN 0-88946-068-X

A CIP catalog record for this book is available from the British Library.

Copyright © 1999 Magnus O. Bassey

All rights reserved. For information contact

<table>
<tr><td>The Edwin Mellen Press
Box 450
Lewiston, New York
USA 14092-0450</td><td>The Edwin Mellen Press
Box 67
Queenston, Ontario
CANADA L0S 1L0</td></tr>
</table>

The Edwin Mellen Press, Ltd.
Lampeter, Ceredigion, Wales
UNITED KINGDOM SA48 8LT

Printed in the United States of America

DEDICATION

This book is dedicated to my parents,
Mr. and Mrs. Bassey Umana Edet,
who educated me through a lot of sacrifice

To Mr. M. U. Umana - my mentor.

TABLE OF CONTENTS

List of Illustrations xi

Foreword xiii

Acknowledgments xv

Introduction xvii

I. NIGERIA: A BRIEF HISTORY 1
    Nigeria: Its Land and Its People, ... 1
    The Early Kingdoms and Empires, ... 2
    The Making of Modern Nigeria, ... 2
    Britain and Modern Nigeria, ... 4
    British Indirect Rule in Nigeria, ... 5
    The Era of Nigerian Independence, ... 8

II. TRADITIONAL EDUCATION IN NIGERIA 11
    Islamic Education in Nigeria, ... 20

III. WESTERN EDUCATION IN NIGERIA 23
    The First Attempt at Western or Formal
    Education in Southern Nigeria, ... 23
    Origins of 19th Century Missions in Nigeria, ... 28
    The Advent of the Church Missionary Society
    (CMS) Into the Nigerian Missionary Field, ... 29
    The Wesleyan Methodist Missionary Society (WMMS), ... 32
    The Baptist Convention of Southern United
    States of America, ... 35
    The Presbyterian Mission, ... 36
    The Catholic Mission, ... 39
    The Vicariate of the Bight of Benin, ... 39
    The Response to Missionary Education in
    Southern Nigeria, ... 40
    The Development of Western Education in
    Northern Nigeria, ... 41

IV. MISSIONARY RIVALRY AND EDUCATIONAL EXPANSION IN
    NIGERIA 1885-1945 61
    The School Revolution in Nigeria, ... 62
    The Roman Catholic Mission and the
    School Revolution in Nigeria, ... 69
    The Founding of Dennis Memorial Grammar

School (DMGS), Onitsha, ... 72
Missionary Rivalry West of the Niger, ... 75
The Results of Church and Christian Missionary
Rivalry in Nigeria, ... 80
Why Christian Missionary Education Was a Dismal Failure in
Northern Nigeria, ... 81
Britain's Laissez-Faire Educational Policy and Its
Consequences for the Nigerian Educational System, ... 84
Colonial Government Intervention in Education, ... 86
Nationalist Governments and the Introduction of the
Universal Primary Education Schemes in the 1950s, ... 88

V. GOVERNMENT TAKE-OVER OF SCHOOLS IN NIGERIA 91
The East Central State Education Edict, 1970, ... 92
Reasons for Government Take-Over of Schools, ... 100
Education as a Fundamental Human Right, ... 100
Education as a Means of Political Socialization, Social and
Economic Development, ... 101
Educational Imbalance between the North and South, ... 103
Educational Imbalance and the Nigerian Civil War, ... 108
Education as an Investment, ... 113
Disparity in Teachers' Conditions of Service, ... 115
Religious Cleavages, ... 118

VI. CONSEQUENCES OF GOVERNMENT TAKE-OVER OF
SCHOOLS IN NIGERIA 119
The Universal Free Primary Education, ... 119
National Policy on Education, ... 121
National Values, ... 124
How to Implement the Policy, ... 124
Language, ... 125
General Overview, ... 126
Consequences of Government Intervention in
Education in Nigeria, ... 126

END NOTES 131

REFERENCES 133

APPENDIX
   The Nigerian 6-3-3-4 System of Education at a Glance 143

INDEX 149

LIST OF ILLUSTRATIONS

TABLES

1. Statistics of Pupils in Nassarawa Schools, 1913 47
2. Education Statistics for Northern Nigeria, 1921 49
3. Number of Church Missionary Society Schools and Scholars in Certain Years 65
4. Number of Wesleyan Schools and Teachers in Various Years 65
5. Number of Roman Catholic Schools West of the Niger in Certain Years 66
6. Enrollment as a Percentage of School-Age Population by Province, 1921-1931 76
7. Number of Schools, Students, and Teachers in Southern Nigeria, by Province and Township, 1921 78
B. Secondary and Teacher Training Institutions Founded in Southern Nigeria, 1859-1930 79
9. Educational Development, Northern and Southern Nigeria 104
10. Primary Enrollments by Sex 105
11. University of Ibadan Output, 1948-1966 107
12. University Population by Regions - 1966 109
13. Student Enrollment Trends in Primary and Secondary Schools 121
14. Trends in Student Enrollment in Nigerian Universities 121

FIGURES

1. Primary School Enrollment, 1912-1965 110
2. Secondary School Enrollment, 1952-1965 111

FOREWORD

Dr. Magnus 0. Bassey provides a fascinating and well-written account of the development of education in Nigeria from pre-Colonial days to Nigerian independence and the eventual government take-over of schools.

By the fifteenth century Islam had become a state religion in much of northern Nigeria. A religion of the book, Islam introduced the reading of the Quran, the writing of Arabic, and the study of Arabic grammar and literature. While Bassey characterizes Islamic education in Nigeria as having been "irregular and poorly organized," it had a lasting influence on Nigerian educational history, especially in its contrasts and conflicts with various forms of Christian missionary education that came later.

The first Europeans to make contact with Nigeria were the Portuguese, who built a church in the late fifteenth century and attempted to convert the ruler of the Benin Kingdom to Christianity. However, the Portuguese efforts failed, inasmuch as they attempted to convert Nigerian adults, rather than educate their children. More successful than the Portuguese were English and French missionaries who, beginning in the early nineteenth century, "were making a virtue out of necessity," as Bassey puts it. Instead of working primarily to convert adults, they perceived that educating Nigerian children was a way to win converts. By training catechists and workers to serve European colonial purposes, a Nigerian middle class began to emerge. On the one side, members of this class owed their status to the missionaries, and in turn they served the colonial ends of the European nations from which the missionaries had come.

Bassey argues that the rapid expansion in education in Nigeria between 1885 and 1945 was the outcome of Church rivalry between Church of England, Protestant sects, and Roman Catholic efforts, rather than an altruistic policy on the part of the several missionary groups. He documents his assertion in various ways, with the result that the reader of his history is persuaded that "until the 1970s the establishment of schools and indeed, Western education itself in many parts of Nigeria was virtually a monopoly of the Christian missions."

After independence several states acknowledged their commitment to a common aim by taking over the mission schools. This action was not an arbitrary or simply an anti-religious decision, but was supported by an appeal to the United Nations Declaration of Human Rights, which holds that everyone has the right to an education. Eventually, the Nigerian commitment to education led to a 6-3-3-4 system (Primary - Junior Secondary School - Senior Secondary School - Higher Education), shaped as a national policy. In acknowledging the rights of all Nigerians to an education, the advocates of national education had to consider the differences between the North and the South of the country, whose educational opportunities had been unequal, due to different historical situations in the two regions. Bassey treats this problem in a systematic way, pointing to the problems involved in the differences and conflicts between the "relatively Islamic educated North" and the "relatively Western educated South."

Bassey's history is a case-study that ends by portraying the struggles of a recently independent nation in its attempts to gain a fundamental sense of a perspective from which the rights of all Nigerians can be recognized, while acknowledging ethnic and religious differences among the nation's people. The educational system that has been painstakingly developed acknowledges the common rights of all its people in the midst of their differences. Bassey tells a story of a nation striving to forge a sense of unity through a national system of education. Perhaps no other nation has a larger place for education in its mission.

J. J. Chambliss
Graduate School of Education, Rutgers University
Editor, Philosophy of Education: An Encyclopedia

ACKNOWLEDGMENTS

This book is an outgrowth of my doctoral dissertation which I submitted to Rutgers, The State University of New Jersey in 1989. I wish to thank specifically the chairperson of my dissertation committee, Dr. J. J. Chambliss, who painstakingly directed my doctoral study; read the final draft of this book and made useful suggestions for improvement and also wrote the Foreword. I must gratefully mention Dr. Reuben N. Choonoo who found time to read parts of the manuscript and Dr. Anthony Roda who read the whole manuscript despite his crowded schedule. I am also grateful to the other members of my dissertation committee, Dr. D. Muschinske and Dr. T. Agbeyegbe, for their contribution towards the completion of my doctoral program.

I am thankful to the statisticians at the Federal Ministry of Education, Science and Technology, Nigeria, for their cooperation during my field research. I thank Mr. Shittu Gambari of Ramat Publishing, Inc., for permission to reproduce the map of Nigeria from his publication, *Destination Nigeria: A Guide to Mixing Business With Pleasure in Nigeria.*

I am most grateful to members of my family for their understanding during the many years of my research and the writing of this book.

To friends and well-wishers who often wondered when this project would become a book, finally, it has ...

INTRODUCTION

The contribution of European missionaries to the development of education in Nigeria has been well documented (Solaru, 1964; Ajayi, 1965; Ayandele, 1967; Afigbo, 1968; Abernethy, 1969; Ekechi, 1972). What has not been equally well documented is the contention that the missionaries were making a virtue of necessity. Education, for the missionaries, was an essential part of their "civilizing" mission because it was a way of winning converts, training African catechists and workers, and creating an African middle class. This book argues that, although education was an important item in the agenda of the missions in Africa, the rapid expansion of education in Nigeria between 1885 and 1945 was actually the accidental outcome of missionary and church rivalry rather than the result of an altruistic policy to provide expanded educational opportunities for the Nigerian populace (Bassey, 1989, 1991).

Until the 1970s the establishment of schools and indeed, Western education itself in many parts of Nigeria was virtually a monopoly of the Christian missions. The missions' interest in education evolved from the missionaries' perceptions of schools as important avenues for conversion. According to Bishop Shanahan, one of the pioneer Catholic missionaries in Eastern Nigeria: "...those who hold the school, hold the country, hold its religion, hold its future" (Abernethy, 1969, p. 41). Father Wauters, a Catholic missionary in Ondo and Ekiti divisions in Yorubaland put the point rather bluntly: "We knew the best way to make conversions in pagan countries was to open schools. Practically all pagan boys ask to be baptized. So, when the district of Ekiti-Ondo was opened (in 1916) we started schools even before there was any church or mission house" (Abernethy, 1969, p. 39). What made educational work even more compelling for missionaries in Nigeria was that, except for small pockets of acceptance, missionaries were neither accepted nor tolerated in most parts of Nigeria. Consequently, missionaries turned their attention to youths and schools as sources of conversion because they soon realized, to their utter dismay and puzzlement, the futility of trying to convert men of good standing in Nigerian society. Indeed, one Roman Catholic missionary lamented:

> For a man of social status to accept Christianity in this country...is to
> expose himself to poverty for the rest of his life; it is to renounce, as
> the Lord asks of the Religious only, his fortune, his future
> and even his family. (Ekechi, 1972, p. 176).

Hence, as Ekechi (1972) claims, "formal education became the bait with which the young generation was enticed to Christianity" (p. 176). Good education, it was believed, would enable young African men to earn a good living as well as exert their own influence and that of their adopted religious denomination upon the society at large.

Evidence abounds in the research literature to show that wherever the Protestant and Catholic missionaries met in Africa, opposition, antagonism, and rivalry flared between them. For instance, the Lutherans were expelled from Abyssinia (now Ethiopia) in 1832 because of Jesuit intrigues. The Jesuits also frustrated the efforts of Johann Krapf (a Lutheran missionary in Abyssinia) and his work among the Gallas in the Kingdom of Shoa in 1844. A. M. Mackay's attempt to spread the gospel among the Ugandans was similarly foiled by Roman Catholic missionaries (Naylor, 1905, pp. 132-133; Oliver, 1967, pp. 5, 6, 67, 74). In Buganda, a French Catholic missionary order called the White Fathers effectively challenged the Anglicans and spread their own brand of evangelical and educational work throughout east and central Africa (Berman, 1975, pp. 13, 21; Oliver, 1967, p. 74; Bassey, 1989, 1991). In Nigeria, however, missionary rivalry was even more intense. Apart from the theological differences, nationality factors came into play. While most of the Protestant missionaries in Nigeria came from England and Scotland, most of the Catholic missionaries came from either France or Ireland. Indeed, France was Britain's greatest rival for colonies in Africa in the 19th century, and Ireland was (and remains to this day) Britain's unruly colony. According to Abernethy (1969): "Intense rivalry began [in Nigeria] during the early years of this century. As both Catholics and Anglicans spread out from their common headquarters...they quickly became engaged in leapfrogging operations" (p. 46).

The year 1885 marks the beginning of the missionary scramble for the souls of Nigerians because after the Berlin Conference of 1884-1885, European nations were required to show evidence of effective occupation for any territory to which they laid claims. Accordingly, soldiers, traders, merchants and missionaries alike were sent afield and used by the various imperial governments to satisfy this clause of the treaty. The result of this scramble was the establishment of unprecedented numbers of schools by the various religious organizations in Nigeria because the schools, unfortunately, became important avenues for proselytization (Bassey, 1989, 1991).

This work offers a new interpretation of the contribution of European missionaries to the development of education in Nigeria. While research in this area has been dominated by loose and heuristic claims about the contributions of European missionaries, this book offers a critical analysis of the behavior of missionaries regarding the education mission field in Nigeria.

The book has six chapters. Chapter one gives a brief history of Nigeria. Chapter two discusses traditional Nigerian education. The chapter argues that although without formal educational institutions, Nigerian societies had developed some means of transmitting their cultures from one generation to the next. The chapter also discusses the inception and significance of Islamic education in Nigeria. Chapter three examines the introduction of Western education to Nigeria. The chapter explores the reasons for the success of Western education in Southern Nigeria as opposed to the North. Chapter four illuminates the state and extent of missionary rivalry in Nigeria between 1885 and 1945. The chapter details the consequences of missionary rivalry for the Nigerian educational system. It concludes that missionary rivalry increased educational opportunities for people in Southern Nigeria but created educational imbalance between the south and the north of Nigeria. Chapter five discusses the reasons for government take-over of schools in Nigeria in the 1970s. Chapter six describes the state of education in Nigeria after government take-over of schools in the country. It concludes that through policy initiatives, Nigerian government has, to a large extent, tried to address the educational imbalance in the country and averted to *some extent* one of the areas of potential conflict.

Source: Shittu Gambari
Destination Nigeria: A Guide to Mixing Business with Pleasure in Nigeria
(Tarrytown, NY: Ramat Publishing Inc., 1997) Reproduced with permission.

CHAPTER I

NIGERIA: A BRIEF HISTORY

Nigeria: Its Land and Its People

Nigeria has a total land area of approximately 356,669 square miles (923, 768 sq km). It is bounded in the Northeast by Chad, in the East by the Cameroons, in the South by the Gulf of Guinea and the Atlantic Ocean, in the West by Benin Republic and in the Northwest by Niger. Nigeria has a population of 98 million (1986 census). The Niger and Benue rivers which are the main waterways in Nigeria converge at a confluence in Lokoja. These rivers divide the country into three major regions, the North, East and West. Each of these regions is dominated by a major ethnic group, the Hausa-Fulani in the North, the Yoruba in the West and the Ibo in the East. However, there are numerous other ethnic groups in Nigeria, each with its own distinct language, customs, religion and political system. For example, in the Eastern region, in addition to the dominant Ibos, there are the Ibibio, the Efik, the Ijaw and the Ibuno. In the North there are the Kanuri, the Tiv, the Bura, the Nupe, the Igala and the Idoma. In the West, in addition to the Yoruba, there are the Edo, the Jekri, the Sobo, the Bini and the Ikaibo.

Nigerians speak several languages and dialects. These languages and dialects have, however, been classified into only a few linguistic groupings. For instance, the Fulani who even though physically belong to the Caucasoid stock speak a language belonging to the Niger-Congo group of languages. The Hausa of Northern Nigeria who are Negroid in physical appearance speak a Hamitic language. The Yorubas and the Edos of Western Nigeria; the Nupes of Northern Nigeria and the Ibos of Eastern Nigeria speak languages belonging to the Kwa sub-family of the Niger-Congo group of languages. (The Twi and Kru-speaking peoples of Ghana are also classified into this group). The Ijo, Kalabari, Okrika, Tiv, Ibibio and Efik of Nigeria all speak languages classified as the Cross River group of the Central Branch, which is often described as Semi-Bantu. The Kanuri of Northeast Nigeria speak a language classified as Central Saharan.

The Early Kingdoms and Empires

Nigeria, the most populous country in Black Africa, was the home of great kingdoms and empires before the advent of the Europeans. The most notable of these kingdoms and empires were the Yoruba Kingdoms of Oyo and Ife, the Benin Kingdom, the Hausa states and the Kanem-Bornu empire.

The Making of Modern Nigeria

European association with Nigeria dates back to the fifteenth century. But for over three hundred years European association with Nigeria was restricted to trade along the coast basically in trading posts and castles. European companies, in trading with Nigeria, operated through chartered companies. Some of the chartered companies included the Royal Niger Company and the West African Company. However, from the beginning of the 19th century, European countries began to lay claims to the African interior. With Britain, France, Germany, Portugal and Italy staking out claims to parcels of African lands, the scramble for Africa had begun in full force during the second half of the 19th century. Accordingly, these countries met from November 1884 to January 1885 under the chairmanship of Prince Otto von Bismarck, the Chancellor of Germany, to lay down rules which governed the scramble for Africa. On February 26, 1885, the Berlin Act was signed. The Act stipulated "that any power which wanted to claim any territory should notify the other signatory powers in order to enable them, if need be, to make good any claims of their own..." and that "any such annexations should be followed by effective occupation before they became valid..." (Boahen, 1966, p. 133). Although in Berlin, the whole African continent had been vaguely partitioned among the various European powers, each European nation had to stake out its claims with effective occupation before they became valid. Consequently, during and after the Berlin Conference, European powers sent out traders, missionaries and soldiers who through bribery, persuasion or coercion caused African rulers to sign protection agreements in which they ceded their lands and their authority to European powers. In this way, African lands were ceded and parceled out according to the political wishes of European powers. In Nigeria, up to 1840, British interest was centered around Lagos, Yorubaland and the Delta coasts. But immediately following the Berlin Conference, Britain claimed a protectorate over the Niger Districts. This area included "the territories on the line of coast between the British Protectorate of Lagos and the right or western bank of the Rio del Rey." It also included the "territories on both banks of the Niger, from its confluence with the River Benue at Lokoja to the sea, as well as the territories on the banks of the River Benue, from the confluence up to and including Ibi" (Crowder, 1966, p. 187). With this acquisition, the British government became entangled in the affairs of Nigeria. In 1866, Britain granted the Niger Company a royal charter. Under the conditions of this charter, the Niger Company acquired political control over all the territories to which it had signed treaties with the chiefs thereby, placing these territories under the protection of the British government. The Niger Company established its headquarters, a constabulary, a high court and an administrative machinery at Asaba to enable it to run the affairs of the territory under its control. With this charter, the Royal Niger Company controlled trade from the Oil Rivers up to Jebba in the hinterlands.

In 1894, Captain Lugard who had an established career as a pioneer of Empire in East Africa was sent to sign a treaty with the ruler of Nikki in Borgu in Nigeria's hinterland on behalf of the British government. At this same time the Royal Niger Company expanded northwards by signing treaties with the Emirs of

Nupe and Ilorin. Due to hotly contested disputes between the British and the French over their West African spheres of influence, Lord Chamberlain, the British Colonial Secretary, decided to create a military force under Captain Lugard to secure the possessions of the Royal Niger Company in the hinterland of Nigeria for the British government. Lugard came back to head the force in 1898. Through a series of negotiations and diplomacy, the British and the French were able to parcel out West African lands without a fight. The British government got most of Nigeria in the deal. In 1891, an effective administration was instituted by Britain over the Oil Rivers Protectorate and Sir Claude Macdonald was appointed governor of that protectorate. In 1893, the Oil Rivers Protectorate became known as the Niger Coast Protectorate. This included all the lands that had made treaties with Britain but were not included in the Royal Niger Company Protectorate. The Niger Coast Protectorate was governed by a Consul General who was responsible to the British Colonial Office.

With time, all the prominent rulers of the Niger and Delta (Jaja of Opobo, Nana, Governor of Benin River, Oba Ovonramwen, the King of Benin) were systematically overrun and deported by British forces. Indeed, with the fall of Benin and the deportation of Oba Ovonramwen to Calabar in September 1897, British subjugation and occupation of Southern Nigeria was almost complete. Earlier in January 1886, Lagos was made self governing. From Lagos, the British launched a series of pacification and punitive measures against Yoruba hinterland and in 1893, Sir Gilbert Carter effectively brought Yorubaland under British control. A British protectorate was declared over Yorubaland with Ibadan as its headquarters.

Britain and Modern Nigeria

In 1899, the Royal Niger Company surrendered its royal charter over the Niger Coast Protectorate to the British government. In 1900, the British government took over responsibility for all territories acquired by the Royal Niger Company. Territories to which the company had signed treaties with the Emirs in the north were formed into the Protectorate of Northern Nigeria. In January 1900, Nigeria was reorganized into three convenient administrative units. These were the Protectorate of Southern Nigeria, Lagos and Protectorate, and the Protectorate of Northern Nigeria. In that same year, the British flag was hoisted in Lokoja. From here on real efforts were made to establish effective British control in Northern Nigeria because even though treaties had earlier been signed with the Emirs of Sokoto and Gwandu these treaties were no more than mere pieces of papers which were good only for diplomacy. Having subdued most of the south, the British maxims moved north because the British were still having difficulty establishing effective administrative control over most parts of Northern Nigeria. The Fulani empires posed serious problems for Lugard's forces. Based on a series of accusations and pretensions ranging from slave raiding, expansionism to decadence of the Fulani administration in Northern Nigeria, Sir Frederick Lugard, the commander of the British forces, launched a series of attacks, first against the Emir of Kontagora and later against Nupe in 1901. Their conquered territories were divided into eight provinces, namely: Borgu, Ilorin, Kabba, Kontagora, Bida, Zaria, Lower Benue and Upper Benue. These territories were placed under Lugard's control. Next, Lugard defeated Yola in 1901, Abuja fell in 1902 and Keffi followed. Kano was captured in January 1903 and on March 14, 1903 Sokoto fell. By 1906, both the north and south of Nigeria were finally pacified, thus marking the beginning of effective British administration in modern Nigeria. Lord Lugard, who was the High Commissioner of Northern Nigeria from 1900 to 1906, returned to Nigeria in 1912 as the Governor-General of the whole country (1912-1919). In 1914, Lugard amalgamated the north and the south of Nigeria.

British Indirect Rule in Nigeria

The British ruled Nigeria, particularly Northern Nigeria, through indirect rule. Indirect rule is governing through pre-existing institutions. The British indirect rule system in Northern Nigeria, though formulated as a matter of expediency, was true in theory as in practice. The reasons which enhanced the principles of indirect rule in Northern Nigeria were:

severe restrictions in funds and personnel; the grip of indigenous monarchs whose authority rested on conquest backed up by effective occupation and the popularly accepted claim that they were indispensable guardians of religion; the Emirs' command of an impressive apparatus of administration, including well developed procedures of direct taxation and an institutionalized judiciary. (Whitaker, Jr. 1970, p. 40).

Perhaps nowhere in the world was the system of indirect rule transformed into a political and moral creed as in Northern Nigeria (Whitaker, Jr. 1970). Ayandele (1980, p. 147) maintains that, "Under Percy Girouard, Lugard's successor, indirect rule became a divine revelation, a sort of natural law, against which it would be dangerous to behave." So much was this creed affirmed that Major Burdon, the Resident Major at Sokoto, declared that the aim of the British was to "rule through existing chiefs, to raise them in the administrative scale, to enlist them on our side in the work of progress and good government" (Whitaker, Jr. 1970, p. 27). He admitted that the British could not rule without native rulers because any attempt to do so would require an army of British magistrates which the present unhealthiness and poverty of the country would not allow. Major Burdon hoped to turn the native rulers into "a high type of British officials, working for the good of their subjects in accordance with the ideals of the British Empire" (Crowder, 1962, pp. 193-194; Whitaker, Jr. 1970, p. 27). The rulers were, however, required to carry "on all that is best in the constitution they have evolved for themselves, the one understood by, and therefore best suited to the people" (Crowder, 1962, pp. 193-194; Whitaker, Jr. 1970, p. 27).

The theory of indirect rule was based on the notion of preserving what was good in traditional institutions (Crowder, 1968, 1978). In Northern Nigeria, more than anywhere else, the British pursued a policy of minimal interference with the local administration and with the duties of the Emirs. Indeed, British officials were required to act as mere advisers to the Emirs and could only interfere with the duties of the Emirs when "their traditional executive authority was questionable" (Crowder,

1978, p. 199). When the British prohibited Christian missionaries from entering certain parts of Northern Nigeria except with the permission of the Emirs, they were conceding to the wishes of the Emirs (Crowder, 1968, p. 136; Callaway, 1987, p. 134).

The point needs to be made that the practice of indirect rule in Northern Nigeria went beyond the wildest imagination of Lord Lugard, its greatest proponent. Hence, when Lugard came back to Nigeria as the Governor-General of the whole country in 1912, he chastised his Lieutenant-Governor, Charles Temple, and some of the leading Residents for delegating too much power to the Emirs and for giving them too much financial autonomy in the native treasury system (Perham, 1965, xli).

So serious was the question of delegation of too much power to the Emirs that Lord Lugard, who never agreed in principle with Sir Donald Cameron, Governor-General of Nigeria from 1931-1935, supported Cameron's efforts to subordinate the status of the Emirs (Perham, 1965). Whitaker points out that the system of indirect rule was so successful in Northern Nigeria that it was adopted in almost all the British territories in Africa (Whitaker, Jr. 1970).

Besides, the power of the Emirs included headship of a large territorial administration -- the emirates. Notice that administrative offices and nonhereditary titles (Sarauta) were held at the discretion of the Emirs who required the incumbents to be loyal and respectful to them, failure of which necessitated severe sanctions, usually the withdrawal of office (Whitaker, 1970). Indeed, in the period between the two world wars, some Emirs ruled as sole native authorities. They were allowed to administer justice according to tradition. They administered their political units as they existed before the advent of the British. They were elected to office by the traditional methods with little interference from the British administration (Crowder, 1978, p. 199). In the Dual Mandate, Lugard maintained that: "The Resident acts as a sympathetic adviser and counselor to the native chief, being careful not to interfere so as to lower his prestige, or cause him to lose interest in his work" (Lugard, 1965, p. 201).

The Era of Nigerian Independence

From 1914 to 1960, Nigeria was ruled by the British. In 1960, Nigeria gained her independence with Sir Abubakar Tafawa Balewa as the first Prime Minister. At this point the country was divided into regions, namely the Eastern Region, the Western Region and Northern Region. A fourth region -- the Midwest -- was created in 1963. Also in 1963, Nigeria became a federal republic. In 1966, a military coup led mostly by easterners toppled the government of Alhaji Tafawa Balewa. Six months later, another coup led by northern officers brought General Yakubu Gowon, a non-Muslim northerner to power. Although General Gowon was able to restore some order after the coup, he was unsuccessful in preventing the massacre of Ibos in Northern Nigeria in 1967 which led the Eastern Region to secede to become the Republic of Biafra. The secession was led by Colonel Odumegwu Ojukwu. This led to a bloody civil war which lasted from 1967 to 1970. In an attempt to ease ethnic tensions in the country, General Gowon increased the number of states in the country to twelve and later on to nineteen. In 1975, another military coup brought General Murtala Muhammed to power. General Murtala Muhammed was assassinated in 1976 and Lt-General Olusegun Obasanjo became head of state. General elections were held in 1979 after a new constitution had been promulgated and Alhaji Shehu Shagari became the second Nigerian civilian Prime Minister. Shagari was overthrown from power by Major General Mohammed Buhari in December 1983 shortly after Shagari's re-election for his second term in office. In August 1985, another coup led by Ibrahim Babangida, the army chief of staff, overthrew Major General Mohammed Buhari. In a bid to ease political, religious and economic tensions, Babangida created a total of eleven additional states in Nigeria. Local government elections were held in 1990 under a two-party system. This was followed by state elections in December 1991 and elections to the national assembly were held in July 1992. However, the presidential election result of June 1993 was annulled by President Babangida. Public pressure forced Babangida to relinquish power in favor of an appointed civilian interim president, Mr. Ernest Shonekan.

General Sani Abacha seized power from Mr. Shonekan on November 17, 1993 with the explanation that he was trying to avoid chaos in Nigeria. General Abacha created six more states in Nigeria in 1996. General Abacha died suddenly in office on June 8, 1998 and was replaced by General Abdulsalaam Abubakar on June 9, 1998. Nigeria is still under military rule.

CHAPTER II

TRADITIONAL EDUCATION IN NIGERIA

Though without schools as formal institutions, traditional[1] African societies had developed some means of creating and transmitting their cultures from one generation to the next. This is so because in order to survive a society must have a way of creating useful citizens and of preparing its youth for the lives they must lead in adult society by providing them with basic minimum skills and for transmitting such skills from one generation to the next. And education is about the only known way of performing this task. It is against this background that we must understand the concept of the method and practice of traditional education in Nigeria in particular and in Africa in general. The system of education practiced in Nigeria and, indeed, in Africa in pre-colonial times is known as traditional education. Traditions are the sum total of the beliefs, opinions, customs, cultural patterns and other ways of life and living which a society passes from generation to generation. In pre-colonial Nigeria, it was the duty of traditional education to sort out worthwhile traditions and to transmit the same from one generation to the next. It is often wondered how traditional education performed these feats, without schools as we know them today. It is to be pointed out, however, that in traditional society, skills, knowledge and attitudes were acquired and transmitted through non-formal institutions. These include parents, age grades, secret societies, etc. (Fafunwa, 1974, pp. 18-19). The aim of traditional education was to "produce an individual who is honest, respectable, skilled, cooperative and conforms to the social order of the day" (Fafunwa, 1974, p. 20). Okonkwo (1985), on the other hand, maintains that "traditional education in Africa...was a cultural action directed at creating attitudes and habits considered necessary for participation and intervention in one's historical process" (p. 104). "Perhaps no educational system," Okonkwo adds, "even in contemporary times, articulated a clearer principle of unity, love and brotherliness between the land and the people and the people themselves" (p. 104). He goes on to say that unity, love and togetherness were highly functional in African society. Indeed, African children are taught from youth to recognize that they are members of an extended family system to which they owe loyalty, respect and affection.

In traditional society, while it was mandatory for the family, both immediate and extended, to educate its offspring in order to make them well adjusted members of the society, education was the responsibility of the entire community (Moumouni, 1968, p. 16). Thus, a child who was not well behaved was considered a disgrace to his family in the first instance and to his clan in the next, because, even though a child bore the names of his immediate family he was *prima facie* a child of the clan. In traditional Nigerian society education was so highly prized that I consider Moumouni's (1968) observation insightful here:

> In the social sphere, even in the feudal societies of pre-colonial Black Africa, education was considered far more valuable than even high birth or fortune, to the point where the title of "man" was inseparable from a certain number of traits linked to education (p. 16).

African education was not compartmentalized and was not cut off from the daily experiences of the learner, for in Africa school and life were the same. Fafunwa (1974) maintains that the main guiding principle of African education was functionalism. He states, "African society regarded education as a means to an end and not an end in itself. Education was for an immediate induction into society and a preparation for adulthood" (p. 15). He summarized the aims, methods and contents of African education as follows:

> ...African education emphasized social responsibility, job orientation, political participation and spiritual and moral values. Children learned by doing, that is to say, children and adolescents were engaged in participatory education through ceremonies, rituals, imitation, recitation and demonstration. They were involved in practical farming, fishing, weaving, cooking, carving, knitting, and so on. Recreational subjects included wrestling, dancing, drumming, acrobatic display, racing, etc., while intellectual training included the study of history, poetry, reasoning, riddles, proverbs, story-telling, story-relays. Education in Africa...combined physical training with character-building and manual activity with intellectual training (Fafunwa, 1974, pp. 15-16).

However, one of the primary concerns of traditional education was its emphasis on social values. Perhaps nowhere is emphasis on social values in traditional education best illustrated than in African literature.[2] In his *No Longer at Ease*, Achebe (1965a) illustrates the spirit of love, unity and togetherness prevalent among Africans by warning: "he that has a brother should hold him to his heart, for a kinsman cannot be bought in the market, neither is a brother bought with money" (p. 129). In a similar view and in the same novel, Achebe (1965a) states that "...a kinsman in trouble had to be saved not blamed, anger against a brother is felt in the flesh not in the bones" (p. 5).

Traditional education also emphasized respect for established traditions, institutions and authority such as respect for the sanctity of marriage. Hence, before the coming of Europeans to Africa, divorce was not commonplace as it is today. Emecheta (1974) demonstrates this fact in her novel, *Second-class Citizen* as follows: "...among our people, there is nothing like divorce or separation. Once a man's wife, always a man's wife until you die. You cannot escape. You are bound to him..." (p. 189). On the same issue Beti (1965) has this to say: "In the old days our ancestors took no cognizance of certain customs now common among us today. Our ancestors did not admit the possibility of a wife leaving her husband" (p. 149).

Traditional education also emphasized endurance, courage and bravery as demonstrated during initiation into secret societies and during the traditional circumcision ceremony which I find instructive to reproduce here; "...I couldn't cry out because...my friends would have thought me a girl. I would have lost my place in the group of boys who are soon to be men" (Oyono, 1974, p. 12). In the same novel but in a different passage, Toundi, the principal character, maintains: "When it started I determined not to cry out. I clenched my teeth and forced myself to think of something" (Oyono, 1974, p. 134). Also, Camara Laye's narrative of the African child's ordeal during the traditional circumcision ceremony is most illuminating here:

> The night of Konden Diara was a strange night, a terrible and miraculous night, a night that passed all understanding...It was a test, a training in hardship, a rite, the prelude to a tribal rite...however great the anxiety, however certain the pain, no one would have dreamed of running away from the ordeal...I knew perfectly well that I was going to be hurt, but I wanted to be a man, and it seemed to me that nothing could be too painful if, by enduring it, I was to come to man's estates. (Laye, 1959, pp.88-94)

In traditional Nigerian society honesty was considered the best policy. Indeed, Fafunwa (1974) maintains that:

> In traditional Nigerian society all parents want their children to be upright, honest, kind and helpful to others and will spare no pain to instill these qualities ...All Nigerian parents, irrespective of ethnic group prefer to remain childless than to have children who will bring shame and dishonour to the family. (p. 24)

In his novel, *A Man of the People*, Achebe (1966) illustrates the need for being a man of honour in traditional society as follows:

> If our people understand nothing else, they know that a man who takes money from another in return for service must render that service or remain vulnerable to that man's just revenge...no juju would save him (p. 136).

And consider this: "Our people have said that a man of worth never gets up to unsay what he said yesterday" (Achebe, 1966, p. 135).

Character building was an uncompromised virtue in traditional society and it formed an important part of traditional education. Indeed, Moumouni (1968) maintains that:

> Moulding character and providing moral qualities are primary objectives in traditional African education. Almost all the different aspects of education of the child and adolescent aim towards this goal, to a greater or lesser degree. In the family, parents concern themselves with the bearing, manners, honesty and integrity of the child. Outside the house, games, the society of his friends in the same age group, and the demands they make on each other, constitute a real source of character building. Sociability, integrity, honesty, courage, solidarity, endurance, ethics and above all the concept of honour are, among others, the moral qualities constantly demanded, examined, judged and sanctioned, in ways which depend on the intellectual level and capacities of the child and adolescent (p. 22).

How was character training developed in youths in traditional society? This was done in three different ways. Firstly, a child was taught directly by his parents and elders the moral requirements of the community, because a child who was not well behaved was considered a disgrace to his family. Hence, children were punished by their parents if they did not benefit from their moral training. Secondly, morality was learned from example especially from those who had acquired experience in public life, native laws and customs and in self discipline. Thirdly, the child learned lessons of morality from the numerous folklores and proverbs often told by parents and other members of the extended family on moral and ethical behavior and on the possible consequences of misconduct. As in most African tales, these proverbs and tales were and still are woven around the tortoise.

Another important feature of traditional education was its emphasis on the development of the physical well-being of the child. This was to enable the child to meet the exigencies of his environment. Notice Okonkwo's admonition of his son Nwoye for his cowardice in *Things Fall Apart*, as follows: "I will not have a son who cannot hold up his head in the gathering of the clan. I would sooner strangle him with my own hands" (Achebe, 1965b, p. 24). However, it should be emphasized that unlike other aspects of traditional education, there was no deliberate effort either by parents or members of the extended family to teach these skills. But, given the open nature of the African topography, children embarked on physical activities to satisfy their natural curiosity and inclinations and in the process exercised their nerves and muscles. African children often engaged themselves in various games and like activities, for instance, jumping, climbing, racing, balancing and swimming, which enabled them to develop their physical well-being. A vital factor in the development of the physique was one's involvement in acrobatic shows and displays -- common features of traditional African dances which the child learned as a matter of course from birth. Hence, without being taught, the African child developed his/her physical self through imitation, intuition, curiosity and in play. Notice the numerous wrestling matches in Achebe's *Things Fall Apart*.

Traditional education also encouraged intellectual training. In traditional society, the child was taught local geography and history right from youth. Indeed, being able to recite one's family tree and genealogy was a must for every male child. Oral history was a matter of prestige for those endowed with the intellectual gift. Parents taught their children plant and animal behavior for protective, cultivation and rearing purposes. Knowledge of the various seasons of the year was a requirement for survival in a purely agrarian society so dependent on the clemency of the weather. Children learned most of their intellectual skills through the process of observation, imitation and participation. Thus by early adolescence children were already conversant with the topography of their community; could distinguish between fertile and infertile lands; between fishing and hunting seasons and knew when to plant their crops and when to harvest them. Through precepts from proverbs, folk-tales, riddles, poetic verses, recitations, games, incantations and praises, the child developed most of his/her reasoning, judgment and mathematical skills. The boys who grew into adults graduated into advanced levels of intellectual training by learning the art of maintaining and retaining their secret cults which to a large extent and to a surprising degree incorporated some elements of social psychology and philosophy.

Within its limitations, traditional education combined manual activity with intellectual training (Moumouni, 1968, p. 24). This was most noticeable in poetic chants of the Yoruba hunters called "Ijala." A. Babalola describes Ijala as,

> The oral poetry of Yoruba hunters and it is one of the various genres of the spoken art of the Yoruba people. It is a type of speech utterance with rudimentary musical characteristics, rather than a species of song. It is a border-line type of spoken art...It is uttered from memory in chanting style but it is essentially a type of verbal art. (Fafunwa, 1974, p. 27).

Awoonor (1975) maintains that, "Ijala artists undergo intensive training from late boyhood and grow by imitation and tuition in medicinal herbs and in the powers of retentive memory" (p. 80). Other professional groups like priests, diviners, herbalists, native doctors, chiefs and cult leaders use poetic chants and incantations in the performance of their duties as well. Poetic chants require considerable intellectual ability indeed since a "recitation can go on for hours with little or no repetition except for the chorus" (Fafunwa, 1974, p. 27). Poetic chants were learned for long periods of time by professionals in order to attain perfection. And as integral parts of their professions, the more one was perfected in them, the more, it was taught, he/she could perform his/her duties successfully. Hence admission to the professions in traditional society was restricted to the intellectually able.

An important aspect of intellectual training was in the area of mathematics. Every ethnic group in Nigeria had developed its own way of counting and numbering long before the advent of the Europeans. Every Nigerian child, for instance, was introduced to counting quite early in life by concrete means, that is, by objects, counting rhymes, folklores, plays and games either at home or in the farms.

Also, special attention was given to vocational education in traditional society. Farming, fishing, trading, hunting and weaving were introduced to children quite early. Most of the occupations, however, were run on an apprenticeship basis. This was a system whereby children were trained, not by their parents, but by master-craftsmen, relatives or friends in their chosen professions in order to maintain discipline and concentration. Serious attention was given to agriculture which was and still is the mainstay of the nation's economy. Agricultural education involved training children to discriminate between fertile and infertile lands. This was a very painstaking exercise indeed since a soil declared unsuitable for one type of crop could be found suitable for another. One way of distinguishing between suitable and unsuitable soil was by dipping the cutlass into the soil. A stony encounter was indicative of a poor soil, unsuitable for deep-rooted crops. A porous soil was suitable for creeping crops. Agricultural education also involved teaching children when and how to set a fire into the bush; how to plant crops; what time to plant them and in what direction? With respect to yam cultivation Ogundijo has this to say:

> There were as many methods [of planting the seeds] as there were crops. Yam was usually cut into sets. Before the father who was also the teacher began to cut the yams, he instructed the children to observe very keenly. Some sets were small while others were big. In each case the teacher explained why certain types were small while others were big. Like a good teacher, he let the children practise with the cutting knives. Anyone who did it very well was praised and those who did not were reprimanded for their failure...Before real planting of the yam sets began, knowledge of arithmetic was again brought into play. The children were made to count the yam sets, usually in groups of two hundred...The yam sets were distributed on the heaps and the boys buried them...(Fafunwa, 1974, p. 32).

Children who had a flair for fishing were apprenticed in fishing boats of family, friends or relatives. There, they were taught navigational techniques including seafaring; the effects of certain stars on tide and ebb; favorable fishing grounds; fish migratorial patterns and habits. Whether it was fishing, farming, trading or weaving, the method was teaching by example and learning by doing. In an interview with a man of years,[3] on the techniques of fishing in traditional society, my informant observed:

> In those days we had no navigational instruments. We followed the sun by day and the moon by night. The position of a certain star could be indicative of a storm or good weather. You only needed to have the eyes to see it and the ability to recognize it. (Interview, August, 1986).

Apart from farming and fishing, children learned trades and crafts. Most important among them were blacksmithing, weaving, wood carving and bronze work. Since these trades needed a high degree of specialization and internship, children were apprenticed for pretty long periods of time but as a rule they were apprenticed outside their parental homes for the simple reason of discipline. Those who took to the professions as -- doctors, priests, village heads, kings, medicine men, diviners, rainmakers, queens and rulers -- underwent long periods of painstaking training and rituals. Mbiti describes the making of medicine men among the Azande which I find most interesting to reproduce here in its entirety:

> In every case, medicine-men undergo formal or informal training. Among the Azande, for example, their training is long and expensive, even starting in the preliminary preparations at the age of five years in some cases. When a young person has made his wishes known that he intends to become a medicine-man he is carefully scrutinized by his would-be teacher, to ascertain that he really 'means business.' Then he is given medicine to eat, which is believed to strengthen his soul and give him powers of prophecy; he is initiated into the corporation by public burial; he is given witchcraft phlegm to swallow; and he is taken to a stream source and shown the various herbs and shrubs and trees from which the medicines are derived.' That is the procedure to becoming a medicine-man among the Azande, but in reality it takes a long time to reach the goal, and it is a complicated affair. Each teacher has his own regulations for his pupils, such as refraining from eating animals like elephants, house rats and various plants, and from sexual intercourse or bathing for several days when one has eaten certain medicines from one's teacher. (Mbiti, 1970, pp. 218-219).

While boys were being trained in the farms, rivers and workshops, the girls were trained by women in homemaking. They were taught how to prepare food, make cloth, care for children, take care of the dwellings and wash utensils. These, they did most often under the strict supervision of their mothers. Girls were sometimes apprenticed to mistresses for certain trades such as dying, weaving and plaiting, the last of which was exclusive for women. Above all, girls were drilled in their future roles as housewives and brides.

Traditional education also concerned itself with community participation and promotion of cultural heritage. In summary, Okonkwo (1985) maintains that:

> traditional education left nothing to chance. It was very well organized, and its curriculum was geared toward achieving the spirit of love and an ordered, rich, and beautiful life...its curriculum emphasized all those virtues and values, ideas and ideals that encouraged healthy growth...the traditional curriculum prepared men against the dangers and challenges of the time and offered them the confidence and the strength to confront those dangers instead of surrendering their sense of self through admission to the decisions of others (p. 106).

Islamic Education in Nigeria

Islam was introduced into parts of present-day Nigeria from about the 10th century A.D. By the 15th century A.D. it had become a state religion in most of Northern Nigeria. It was a state religion in Bornu in 1085; in Kano between 1349 and 1385; in Katsina between 1320 and 1352. It is believed that Islam reached Yorubaland at about the close of the 18th century (Fafunwa, 1974, p. 57). Hand in hand with the introduction of Islam into parts of Nigeria came the introduction of Islamic education because Islam as we know it is a religion of the book -- the Quran. Thus, to be a good Muslim one must be able to read and write Arabic -- the language of the Quran. To the ardent Muslims then, the teaching of the Quran was providential, for "one of the Islamic traditions states that the best man among you is one who learns the Quran and then cares to teach it" (Fafunwa, 1974, p. 55).

Islamic education was carried out in three stages in Nigeria. The first stage was the piazza which is the equivalent of our present primary school. It was meant for children, beginning between the ages of five and six. The course of study lasted for between five and seven years (Gbadamosi, 1967, p. 87). Though the classes at this level of Islamic education were often very large, the teachers lived on charity or on student donations because they were not paid employees. In most instances, however, the teachers had other vocations from where they earned their living. At this stage the school day lasted from 8 am to about 12 noon. Another session might begin from about 1 pm to about 6 pm and, occasionally there was a third session which went right into the night. The school day in actuality varied from school to school, according to the vocation of the teacher. Here the pupils learned chapters of the Quran by repetition and by rote. Pupils were told about the life and times of Prophet Muhammad and some Islamic history. They were taught how to be good Muslims by the example of their teacher, and by precepts. They also often went with him from place to place on his preaching tours and sometimes stayed with him in his home. The education at this stage was largely informal and the pupils took part in other activities including drills on how to pray, worship and above all the tenets of the religion.

At the completion of the first stage of his education, the pupil moved on to the next stage which is the tablet or beginners stage -- Makarantar Allo (Fafunwa, 1974, p. 55). At this stage the pupil carried out a systematic course of study which included learning Arabic characters and alphabets as well as learning to read the first two parts of the Quran. At the end of this stage, the student progressed into the next -- Makarantar Ilmi which consists of learning Arabic grammar, literature and poetry; the study of the Hadith, Tafsir and Islamic Law and, best of all, the translation of the Quran (Gbadamosi, 1967, p. 91). Other courses of study at this level of education also include logic, arithmetic, astrology, divination and medicine. Though teachers in Makarantar Ilmi were generally more qualified, like other groups of Muslim teachers they were generally not paid officials.

At the completion of the Ilmi stage, however, the pupil may opt for a specialized course of study at any of the Islamic Universities at Fez, Sankore, Timbuctu or Al-Azhar in Cairo (Fafunwa, 1974, p. 62). He may also decide to study locally in any one of the Islamic learning centers in Nigeria under very renowned Islamic scholars. From this system of education scholars, teachers and religious reformers were produced. It was also the educational system that produced judicial, clerical and administrative personnel for Northern Nigeria before the advent of colonialism.

However, in spite of Fafunwa's (1974) contention that "it was Islam that revived the human pursuit of science" and that "it was through the Arabs and not the Romans that the modern world achieved light and power through science," Islamic education in Nigeria was irregular and poorly organized and could not meet the needs of the modern technological and scientific age. The status of Islamic teachers was generally poor. Indeed, Fafunwa himself cares to admit:

> This noble principle (the principle in which teachers depended on charity) which was successfully applied in the early stage of the development of Islamic education, reduced the status of a teacher (Muallim) to that of a mere beggar: he came to occupy socially a rather low status. He had to wander from place to place looking for charitable Muslims to patronize and give him food and shelter. Whenever his efforts were not sufficient to procure the bare necessities of life, he had to send his pupils from door to door asking for charity. (Fafunwa, 1974, p. 55)

On the qualifications of the Islamic teachers, Fafunwa (1974) notes:

> The qualifications of Quranic school teachers differ from person to person and from place to place. Sometimes they are highly learned Ulama, well versed in Islamic studies, but this is rare. Then there are those whose only qualification is that they can recite the Quran and write Arabic characters. (p. 64)

CHAPTER III

WESTERN EDUCATION IN NIGERIA

The First Attempt at Western or
Formal Education in Southern Nigeria

For the most part what came to be known as formal or Western education in Southern Nigeria[4] was provided primarily by Christian missionary bodies and associations. The Portuguese were the first Europeans to make contacts with Nigeria. In 1472 Portuguese merchants and missionaries visited Benin and Lagos in Nigeria. After the establishment of Fort Elmina in 1482, the Portuguese built a church for the Africans there. In 1486 a Portuguese explorer and merchant, John Affonso d'Aveiro, visited Benin (Ryder, 1969, p. 30). Benin established economic, political and religious ties with Portugal. Trade in ivory, beads, cloths and firearms developed. Diplomatic relations were established between the two countries and the Benin embassy led by the Ohen[5] of Ughoton represented Benin in Portugal. In 1516 when John Affonso again visited Benin, he persuaded the Oba[6] to become a Christian for if he did his country would become better. At first, the Oba seemed well-disposed to the religion. Hence, he sent Ohen Okun of Gwatto as his representative to the King of Portugal requesting the Portuguese monarch to send priests who would teach him and his people the faith. The Oba also requested arms. He requested Christianity and arms at the same time because he was well aware of the Papal decree which forbade the delivery of arms to unbelievers (Ryder, 1960, p. 1).

However, the King of Portugal replied by sending Roman Catholic priests, some presents, church vestments, books and altar furnishings but without the arms which "he refused to send until the Oba should prove the sincerity of his professed inclination to Christianity" (Ryder, 1961, p. 234). In a letter to the Oba of Benin, King Manuel of Portugal explained his action in the following words:

> ...Therefore, with a very good will we send you the clergy that you have asked for; they bring with them all the things that are needed to instruct you and your people in the knowledge of our faith. And we trust in Our Lord that He will bestow His grace upon you, that you may confess it and be saved in it for all the things of this world pass away and those of the other last forever. We earnestly exhort you to receive the teachings of the Christian faith with that readiness we expect from a very good friend. For when we see that you have embraced the teachings of Christianity like a good and faithful Christian, there will be nothing in our realms with which we shall not be glad to favour you, whether it be arms or cannon and all other weapons of war for use against your enemies; of such things we have a great store, as Dom Jorge your ambassador will inform you. These things we are not sending you now, as he requested, because the law of God forbids it so long as you are...(Ryder, 1961, pp. 234-235)

John Affonso and the missionaries settled down in Benin to carry out evangelization and educational works. They built churches at Ogbelaka, Idumwerie and Akpakpava (Egharevba, 1960, p. 28). By 1516, the Oba sent his sons and those of the other chiefs to be baptized and "taught to read by the missionaries" (Ryder, 1961, p. 235). Duarte Pires, a Portuguese then living in Benin, maintained that reading lessons in Portuguese made very satisfactory progress (Ryder, 1961, p. 235). Ironically, the Oba was not himself converted "because he needed leisure for such a deep mystery as this" (Ryder, 1961, p. 235). Before John Affonso died, a few thousand people were baptized in Benin. And in the 1570s, the Portuguese missionaries established a school for the training of Africans as priests and teachers on the island of Sao Thome near the Nigerian coast (Fafunwa, 1974, p. 74).

By the turn of the century, however, missionary endeavor and by implication education enterprise collapsed in Benin like the Biblical walls of Jericho because the Oba of Benin was interested in arms and education for his people and not in Christianity. Ryder (1969) explains the Oba's desire for arms as follows:

> At the time he sent his envoys to Portugal, the Oba found himself hard-pressed by his enemies and was clearly intent on obtaining firearms, which would have given him a decided military advantage. He had seen these weapons in the hands of the Portuguese, and had probably heard that they were supplied to the Christian King of the Congo. Baptism, as the Portuguese repeatedly stressed to him and to other princes, would bring him guns as well as grace. (p. 46)

Indeed, the Oba of Benin's quest for arms rather than Christianity was confirmed by de Barros when he said that "he sought the priests rather to make himself powerful against his neighbours with our favour than from a desire for baptism" (Ryder, 1969, p. 46). Apart from non cooperation, Portuguese missionaries failed to a large extent because they directed their efforts and energy at converting the Oba first in the hope that if he were converted his subjects would follow suit, judging from the fact that the Oba was adored and feared by his subjects. This notion of the divine rule of kingship was enhanced by the absolute authority possessed by the Obas of Benin as illustrated by a Portuguese merchant thus:

> The Kings are worshiped by their subjects, who believe they come from heaven and speak of them always with great reverence, at a distance and on bended knees. Great ceremony surrounds them, and many of these Kings never allow themselves to be seen eating, so as not to destroy the belief of their subjects that they can live without food... (Crowder, 1966, p. 71)

Based on a wrong premise of the divine Kinship in Benin, the Italian and Spanish Capuchin missionaries went straight into attempting to convert the Oba in 1651. However, they were given rooms in the Oba's palace but were not allowed access to the Oba. Indeed, the party was allowed to see the Oba only twice in ten months and even on these occasions they were denied the services of interpreters. Worse still, during their stay, they tried to disturb a religious festival which led to their deportation (Ryder, 1961, p. 245; Ajayi, 1965, p. 3). Explaining their failure in

Benin one of the Capuchins noted:

> The reason why these negroes cannot embrace the Faith, as they would wish to do, is that they consider themselves slaves of their King and would not dare to become Christians until the King himself is converted. (Ryder, 1961, p. 247)

This assertion confirms an earlier one by Father Columbin of Nantes that:

> The King is so greatly feared by his subjects that when they but hear his name spoken, they all fall prostrate and adore him with fear and unbelievable reverence. Thus from this it may be imagined that if the King were converted to the Faith, the rest of his subjects would easily be won over. (Ryder, 1961, p. 241)

However, as missionaries themselves were to discover later, they were greatly mistaken in their divine rule theory, for as Ryder has pointed out:

> ...the Oba was held in thrall by a ceremonial religion, apart from which he could exercise but little influence over his people. It may well be doubted whether even at a time when the Oba had wielded considerable political power, as in 1515, he could, by his will alone, have abandoned the religion of his State. (p. 247)

Furthermore, the missionaries placed so much emphasis on the ability of the King to convert his people despite the fact that at this time religion was becoming more and more individualistic. Religion was considered a personal rather than a communal affair in Benin at this time. (Ajayi, 1965, p. 2).

In Warri, on the contrary, the Olu[7], eager to retain his independence from Benin, courted the friendship of and hankered after the Portuguese in the 1570s. Thus, he declared the doors of his Kingdom open to the Augustinian missionaries from Sao Thome. One of the Olu's princes, an Itsekiri, was baptized as Sebastian. Sebastian later sent one of his sons, Domingos 1 to study in Portugal for eight years where he got married to a Portuguese lady who gave birth to his successor Dom Antonio Domingos. When Dom Antonio became the Olu, he was the crusader for the spread of Christianity among his subjects. But in spite of this royal patronage, Christianity in Warri thrived only in the court of the King. It was the failure of

Christianity in Warri which prompted the Bishop of Sao Thome to write in 1620, saying:

> Outside the small town of Santo Agostinho there are no other Christians; and even in the town only a minority are of the Catholic faith. Although very many of them are nominally Christian, true Christianity is almost wholly confined to the King and the Prince (i.e., Dom Domingos); the rest only call themselves Christians in order to please the King. They take their children to baptism only with the greatest reluctance, believing that a baptized child will die immediately. The majority of them take wives without the sacrament of matrimony, they circumcise their children and practice superstitious rites and sorcery. (Ryder, 1960, p. 8)

Other factors which hindered the spread of Christianity and education in Nigeria at this time were language difficulties, transportation problems, health problems, inadequate number of missionaries, doctrinal differences and, above all, missionaries who were more concerned with the Christian doctrine than with secular education (Ajayi, 1965, p. 6). But as events in later missionary endeavors were to show, schools became important avenues for the spread of Christianity. Finally, the fortunes of education in Nigeria were affected by the nearly three hundred years of slave trade. One may wonder why I have taken this much time analyzing the failure of Christianity in Benin and Warri instead of education. The point I earlier made is worth reiterating here: that up to the 1970s, Christian missionaries were harbingers of Western or formal education in most parts of Southern Nigeria. Notice A. F. Leach's assertion that:

> The missionaries had to come with the Latin service-book in one hand and the Latin grammar in the other.(Because) not only had the native priests to be taught the tongue in which their services were performed, but their converts...had to be taught the elements of grammar before they could grasp the elements of religion. So the grammar school became in theory, as it often was in fact, the necessary ante-room, the vestibule of the Church... (Fafunwa, 1974, p. 81)

This was as true in England as it was in Nigeria. With particular reference to

Nigeria, Sir James Robertson summed it all up in 1956 when he wrote:

> The growth of social services in under-developed territories of Asia and Africa, has been due in a large measure to the devotion and endeavor of Christian Missionaries. This is very true of Nigeria which is greatly indebted to missionary effort for the foundation of its medical and educational services. The state was at first slow to assume responsibilities in this sphere... (Afigbo, 1968, p. 198)

The failure of the missions, therefore, affected the fortunes of education in Nigeria in an important and decisive manner during the first missionary encounter with Nigeria.

The Origins of 19th Century Missions in Nigeria

Following the evangelical revival movements in Europe during the late 18th century, missionary fervor, dormant since the 15th century, was rekindled regarding the largely unrewarding endeavor of evangelizing the Nigerian interior. The European evangelical movement was due largely to the work of John Wesley. Wesley's challenge to the established Anglican Church led to the anticlerical and evangelical movements and, consequently, to the "Protestant Awakening" which swept across Europe and America in the 19th century. This awakening demanded renewed zeal and commitment on the part of individual Christians as well as deep concern for the personal act of conversion. It was Wesley's message that strengthened the desire for missionary work (Bassey, 1991).

The work of a group of influential Victorian Englishmen known as the Clapham Sect was responsible for the formation of one of the first Protestant missionary societies to venture into Nigeria. Prominent members of the Clapham Sect included William Wilberforce, Granville Sharp, and Zachary Macaulay. In 1799 these men and others formed the Church Missionary Society (CMS) as an evangelical arm of the Church of England. Other missionary groups represented in Nigeria were the Wesleyan Methodist Missionary Society (WMMS), the Presbyterian Church of Scotland, the Baptists from the (American) Southern Baptist Convention, and the Society of African Missions (the Catholic Mission) from France (Bassey, 1991).

The Advent of the Church Missionary Society (CMS) Into The Nigerian Missionary Field

The CMS ventured into the Nigerian missionary field as a result of the advocacy of one of its members, Thomas Fowell Buxton, a prominent member of Parliament and a Vice President of the society. It was Buxton, who in his book *African Slave Trade and its Remedy*, advocated the regeneration of Africa by "calling forth her own resources." He urged the abolition of the nefarious slave trade at its roots by exploring the Niger into its hinterlands, negotiating treaties with the natives and establishing peaceful trade with the inhabitants. Buxton argued that if Christianity, commerce and civilization (by "civilization", the Victorians meant British culture and control) were pursued, slave trade would be destroyed and civilization would be achieved naturally through cause-and-effect. He noted that by introducing commerce, civilization and Christianity, a blow would be struck at the nefarious traffic in human beings from which slave trade could not recover. The British government, he maintained, would acquire cheap raw materials, new markets, increased productivity, employment and profits in return (Webster, 1963:418). Consequently, Buxton urged the cooperation of government and the missionary societies in the deliverance of Africa. He, in short, believed that the Bible and the Plough would regenerate Africa. In his book he noted:

> We must elevate the minds of her people and call forth the resources of her soil...Let missionaries and schoolmasters, the plough and the spade, go together and agriculture will flourish; the avenues to legitimate commerce will be opened; confidence between man and man will be inspired; whilst civilization will advance as the natural effect, and Christianity operate as the proximate cause, of this happy change. (Buxton, 1839, pp.282 & 511).

Education of Africans was indeed in the agenda of the missionary societies. As one of the outstanding members of the CMS (and its later General Secretary) Henry Venn, maintained in 1857, by restructuring the economy of Africa in favor of legitimate trade, a new generation of enlightened educated African middle-class elites would emerge in the church, commerce, industry and politics. According to Venn, these elites might "form an intelligent and influential class of society and become the founders of a Kingdom which shall render incalculable benefits to Africa and hold a position among the states of Europe" (Webster, 1963, p. 420). It was Venn's desire for the Church to prepare Africans for leadership. Indeed, after the disastrous 1841 Niger expedition, Henry Venn urged that a "full scale Africanization of the church had to begin since Europeans could not withstand death from malaria and other tropical diseases."[8] And in February 1842, the CMS committee resolved that:

> adverting to afflictive results of the Niger Expedition...the committee are of opinion that further measures should be adopted in order to train natives in Sierra Leone with a view to their being employed as teachers of their own countrymen... (Solaru, 1964, p. 10)

At the request of Sierra Leone ex-slaves for missionaries to teach their countrymen the gospel, a party of CMS missionaries led by Henry Townsend arrived at Badagry from Sierra Leone on the 17th of December, 1842 (Solaru, 1964, p. 3). Others who accompanied Townsend on this trip were two Sierra Leone ex-slaves, Andrew Wilhelm and John McCormack. After a brief visit to Abeokuta, the CMS party returned to Sierra Leone in 1843, leaving Andrew Wilhelm to take care of the newly established mission station at Badagry. But shortly after, in 1845, a ship load of CMS missionaries, teachers and lay workers arrived in Badagry. The party consisted of three missionaries and their families, Mr. and Mrs. Samuel Ajayi Crowther, Rev. and Mrs. Henry Townsend, Rev. and Mrs. Gollmer; two school teachers, Messrs. William Marsh and Edward Phillips; four carpenters, three laborers, two servants and one interpreter, Mr. Willoughby. Within their eighteen month stay in Badagry the party established a mission station, a school and a mission house. Rev. Henry Townsend was placed in charge of the school. Still, while in Badagry the CMS set up an industrial program there. B. W. Hodder maintains that:

> The Church Missionary Society had vegetable gardens and crop fields down by the Lagoon in the 1840s; and was responsible for introducing swamp rice and onion cultivation into the area. Crowther...sought to encourage agriculture in many ways. He had forest land cleared and cultivated; he introduced the plough, and

instituted prizes for the best farms. (Oduyoye, 1978, p. 258)

The CMS party proceeded to Abeokuta in August 1846 leaving Rev. Gollmer to take charge of the mission and to keep up communications with Abeokuta. Messrs. Edward Phillips and William Marsh were left in charge of the school. In 1853, the CMS opened a station in Ibadan. In all their new stations the CMS missionaries opened day schools while their wives took charge of the girls. Sunday schools were run for both boys and girls where they were taught to read the Bible. Indeed, in 1861, there were sixty-five children in CMS schools in Abeokuta. Industrial education for trades like carpentry, blacksmithing and agriculture were encouraged.

At Ibadan, Rev. and Mrs. Hinderer opened a school for children and on the 19th of May, 1853, Anna Hinderer reported as follows:

> We have now a nice little day school. Some having come very regularly, I gave them blue shirts yesterday, and it was a pretty sight this morning to be greeted by nine blue boys. I have also now four children given me, but as our house is small, and they like to go home at the end of the day we let them. They are here early enough in the morning; a little boy and girl of Olunloyo's; a boy whose father has been quite an enemy of ours; and a little boy without parents, the brother of our schoolmaster. (Oduyoye, 1978, p. 270)

In Abeokuta, the CMS intensified their educational program such that by 1864 there were 3,000 literate people who had passed through CMS schools (Solaru, 1964, p. 4). However, attention was particularly paid to the training of catechists and teachers. Thus, in 1859 a Teacher Training Institution was founded there. In 1867 this institution was removed to Lagos following an outbreak of violence against Europeans and their subsequent expulsion from Abeokuta. "The Training Institution and the Female Institute formerly at Abeokuta were established in Lagos where the former became known as the Lagos Training Institution, and the CMS Grammar School" (Solaru, 1964, p. 4). This girls' school also prepared girls for the teaching profession. The Training Institution was moved into a new location with Rev. (later

Bishop) Isaac Oluwole as the first African principal. Rev Oluwole set the tone of the institution as being; "...to produce Christian boys, diligent, obedient, straightforward, kind, evidently God-fearing; the number of...(which) will increase as Christian homes increase" (Solaru, 1964, p. 4).

In 1896, the Training Institution was removed to Oyo and its main objective from now on was to produce teachers. At Oyo, the Institution started with ten students but the number soon rose to seventeen in 1897. At Easter 1900, the first valedictory was held in which five students were appointed to work in different parts of Yorubaland. By 1904, twenty-nine teachers had been produced from the Institution and were catering to more than 700 pupils (Solaru, 1964, p. 5). The composition of students in the institution varied, coming as they did from the East, West and Northern parts of Nigeria. Indeed, there was a student from the Gold Coast (now Ghana) in the institution.

In 1859, Rev. T. B. Macaulay founded the Lagos Grammar School and the first female institution for CMS girls in Lagos was founded in 1872. On the whole:

> The CMS...sent some students abroad for technical education--brick and tile making, navigation, horticulture, industrial management and established a few 'industrial institutions' locally...One was established at Abeokuta in 1851. It collected and cleaned cotton for export, taught brickmaking, carpentry and printing...But these always remained modest attempts and did little more than produce masons and carpenters to build missionary houses and coffins...While these have disappeared, the CMS Grammar School at Lagos which was founded contrary to CMS convictions had continued to flourish. (Ajayi, 1963, p. 519)

The Wesleyan Methodist Missionary Society (WMMS)

The Methodist Mission was brought into the Nigerian educational scene by liberated Sierra Leone ex-slaves in Freetown who by 1839 had begun to return to their original homeland in Nigeria. A Liberian newspaper, *Monrovia Africans' Luminary*, published news of the emigration of one of the freed slaves in its edition of July 2, 1841 as follows:

> He (James Fergusson) was a native of Aku (Yoruba) country. He was taken as a slave, recaptured and brought to the Methodist Church, and received a measure of education. This man with a number of his countrymen having amassed some wealth, determined to return to his own country. They purchased a vessel at Sierra Leone and hired a white man to navigate her, and went to Badagry. And now having reached his fatherland in safety he writes for a missionary to the honoured individual through whose instrumentality ...he had himself become a Christian. (Solaru, 1964, p. 2)

Rev. Thomas Dove, a Wesleyan missionary whose pastoral jurisdiction was then in Freetown, gave an account of the emigrants to his headquarters in London in the following words:

> ...most of these bold enterprising men are useful members of our society. They have taken down elementary schoolbooks, slates, Bibles and Testaments for the purpose of making a beginning in that land... (Solaru, 1964, p. 2)

Shortly after their return to their original homelands, the emigrants petitioned the Queen of England, urging her to send missionaries to come and teach their brothers and sisters. The following letter from James Fergusson attests to the desire of the Sierra Leone emigrants for the education of their countrymen:

> ...So I humbly beseech you, by the name of the Jehovah to send one of the messengers of God to teach us more about the way of salvation because I am now in a place of darkness where no light is. It is to bring our fellow citizens into the way which is right... And as I know better than them, it is my duty to put them right... Some of my family--children who arrive by the brig Margaret--wishes the children to be instructed also. So I humbly beg of you...send us one of the servants of Christ to instruct us; by so doing, if we ourselves are well instructed, I will speak to them the same as I have been instructed... (Solaru, 1964, p. 2)

This letter, it is said, was countersigned by Waratu, a chief in Badagry (Solaru, 1964, p. 2). Another Sierra Leone ex-slave is reported to have written to Rev. Thomas Dove, the resident Methodist Minister in Sierra Leone, saying:

> For Christ's sake, come quick. Let nothing but sickness prevent you...come, see God convert the heathen... Do not stop to change

> your clothes, to eat, to drink, or sleep, and salute no man by the way.
> Do, do, for God's sake, start at this moment; do not neglect me with
> all this burden, it is more than I can bear. (F. Deaville Walker, cited
> in Fafunwa, 1974, p. 78)

In his correspondence with his home office, Rev. Dove maintained that the emigrants wanted:

> ...the Gospel of God our Savior...(to) be preached unto her, that
> schools may be established, that Bibles may be sent, that the British
> flag may be hoisted, and that she may rank among the civilized
> nations of the earth. (Ajayi, 1965, p. 30)

The first group of missionaries to respond to the call of the emigrants were the Wesleyan Methodists. It was the Wesleyan Methodist Mission that sent Thomas Birch Freeman from the Gold Coast to Badagry on September 24, 1842. Freeman was accompanied in the trip by William de Graft. They took with them some timber for the building of the mission house. In December, Freeman traveled to Abeokuta at the invitation of the Oba, Sodeke, because most of the emigrants were settled there. Returning to Badagry on Christmas Eve, Freeman met Rev. Townsend of the CMS who had arrived there on December 17, 1842 on a similar mission.

The Wesleyan Methodists were the first to establish a school in Badagry. Mr. and Mrs. de Graft, who established this school, called it "Nursery of the Infant Church", because they considered it the training ground for the church. Freeman, for one, believed that:

> The school...is training ground. The children are to be trained to
> become Christians and thus help the church to grow. Christianity and
> Western Education go hand in hand. Birch Freeman believed that no
> good education can be effected without a good Christian religious
> training. (Cookey-Gam, 1980, p. 6)

Thomas Freeman returned to the Gold Coast, leaving de Graft in charge of the school. In 1844, however, Rev. Samuel Annear and his wife replaced Mr. and Mrs. de Graft. In 1876, the Wesleyan Mission founded the Methodist Boys' High School in Lagos and in 1879 the Methodist Girls' High School was founded. With the increase in primary schools, the Wesleyans felt the need for teacher training. In 1903, the Wesleyan Methodist Committee resolved to open an institution for the training of teachers and catechists. This institution was established in 1905 at Ibadan and was designed to train teachers who would receive an education that would fit them for employment in the elementary schools.

The Baptist Convention
of Southern United States of America

The Baptists were operating in Liberia from about 1822. Thus, following the success story of the Sierra Leone emigrants to Nigeria, some of the freed slaves in Liberia, who included among them some Baptists, also found their way to Nigeria. However, the pioneer work of this mission in Nigeria was that of Thomas Jefferson Bowen, a young American evangelist who arrived in Badagry in August 1850. Having read William de Graft's account of the conversion of old Simeon of Igboho, he was determined to compete with other missionary bodies in the evangelization of foreign lands (Ayandele, 1968, p. xii-xiii; Cookey-Gam, 1980, p. 7). T. J. Bowen was determined to go to the Sudan or Central Africa.[9] to carry out a "Niger Expedition" in line with that of 1841 carried out by the British and the Church Missionary Society or at least to get to Igboho. Due to political unrest in the interior, Bowen halted his efforts to penetrate inland. He instead stayed at Abeokuta as the guest of the CMS missionary, Henry Townsend and the Oba, for eighteen months learning the language and familiarizing himself with the environment. Bowen later settled down at Ijaye. Of all the foreign missionaries, Bowen's zeal in the education of Africans was most succinctly demonstrated. In 1857 he wrote:

> We desire to establish the Gospel in the hearts and minds and social life of the people, so that truth and righteousness may remain and flourish among them, without the instrumentality of foreign missionaries. This cannot be done without civilization. To establish the Gospel among any people they must have Bibles, and therefore must have the art to make them, or the money to buy them. They must read the Bible and this implies instruction...To diffuse a good degree of mental culture among the people, though a secondary

object, is really and necessarily one part of missionary work in Africa; and he that expects to evangelize the country without civilization will find, like Xavier in the East and the Jesuits in South America, and the priests in Congo, that his labors will end in disappointment. (Bowen, 1857, pp. 322-323)

Bowen, like Buxton before him, believed that the whole social existence of the African would be changed with the emergence of eminent scientists, merchants, technocrats, intellectuals and intelligent rulers. Consequently, he believed that Christianity will only be implanted in Yorubaland and indeed in Nigeria when these categories of people are produced through civilization or education (Ayandele, 1968, p. xxxv). Bowen was committed to the study of the Yoruba language because he wanted "to make the grammar as perfect as possible, exhibiting in a condensed form every role to be observed in writing and speaking pure idiomatic Yoruba" (Ayandele, 1968, p. xiv). Bowen produced his famous Grammar and Dictionary of the Yoruba language in 1862. In 1885 the Baptists founded the Baptist Academy in Lagos.

The Presbyterian Mission

At the height of the missionary zeal in the mid 19th century, the Presbyterian Church of Scotland had an eye on the evangelization of some parts of Africa. Consequent upon consultations, the missionaries decided to direct their efforts to Calabar. A letter was thus sent through Captain Turner, an English trader who was well-known in Calabar to the chiefs and peoples. In his reply of January 1843, Turner wrote of the favorable disposition of the Calabar Chiefs to receiving missionaries and education. And in a reply to an enquiry about the possibility of establishing missions and schools in Calabar, Turner replied that the King and Chiefs of Calabar had stated:

The land will be at your service...it will be guaranteed to its occupants for ever...the King and Chiefs say they are desirous of your coming among them...hoping to have their children taught in English learning. (Solaru, 1964, p. 12)

Indeed, a month earlier the chiefs of Calabar had signed a treaty with a

Queen's ship to abandon slave trade and to receive missionaries. However, having agreed to abolish slave trade, the people of Calabar made the following demands from their associates:

> ...now we settle treaty to not sell slaves...we must have too much man for country and want something for make work and trade. And if we could get seed for cotton and coffee...and if some men come teach we way for do it...and then some men must come for teach book proper, and make all men saby God like white man, and then we go for same fashion. (Solaru, 1964, p. 12)

As a matter of fact, when Captain Owen wrote to the Colonial Office in April 1829, it was on the same note that he sounded--an insatiable quest for learning or formal education by the people of Calabar. Hence he stated in his memo that the people of Calabar wanted:

> to be instructed in the methods of making sugar and to obtain the necessary machinery for which they say they have repeatedly applied to their friends in Liverpool without success. For these advantages they are ready to pay handsomely. (Ajayi, 1965, p. 54)

Ajayi (1965) adds that:

> What distinguished Calabar from the rest (of the Delta city-states) was the length and depth of its attachment to English traders. English was the only European language spoken by Calabar traders, and Hope Waddell found 'Very intelligible journals of the affairs of this kept by its rulers, written in English, of so old a date as 1767.(p. 53)

On April 10, 1846, Rev. Hope Masterton Waddell arrived at Calabar with a party of Presbyterians comprising Samuel Edgerley, an English printer accompanied by his wife; Andrew Chisholm, a carpenter, Edward Miller, an African teacher and George, an ex-slave boy. On arrival, Hope Waddell met with the paramount ruler of Calabar, King Eyo and his chiefs. One remarkable thing on this occasion was that Hope Waddell and his party discovered that King Eyo and his sons were literate. Indeed, Hope Waddell realized that neither the teacher nor carpenter he had brought with him could match the competence of the royal couple in the 3R's (Fafunwa, 1974, p. 80).

Hope Waddell started in Calabar in 1846 with a little congregation largely made up of slave converts; men who suffered from social disabilities--lepers, widows, the poor and the infamous. From here, however, the congregation began to grow. One of the greatest contributions of the Presbyterian mission in Calabar was in the area of industrial training. The proposal to establish an industrial training institution in Calabar was first made by Rev. Samuel Edgerley in 1879. The proposal included the training of clerks, messengers, engineers, carpenters, bricklayers, tailors, blacksmiths, painters, etc. However, it was through the advocacy of Mary Slessor that the proposal received the support of the Church of Scotland in 1892. Thereafter, a team comprising Dr. Robert Laws of Livingstonia and the Rev. W. Risk Thomas from Jamaica was sent to establish contacts and make arrangements with the Calabar committee for the establishment of the proposed industrial institution with the following aims: "(a) the training of apprentices from elementary schools in different trades and (b) the training of teachers and pastors" (Solaru, 1964, p. 13). Since the Government recognized the importance of such an institution it proposed the addition of a school for the provision of "advanced instruction in Calabar as embodied in education rules" (Solaru, 1964, p. 13). However, the Government was to bear the cost for such a building which was to house the additional institution in addition to giving an annual grant of £200 to maintain the Industrial Department.

The progress of the Hope Waddell Training Institution, named after the pioneer Presbyterian missionary, was very rapid and according to the Government report of 1906, "continued to supply the educational needs of Calabar and District, and at Creek Town, near Calabar" (Nwabara, 1977, pp. 60-61). Indeed, by this time the school was occupying five buildings erected by the government at a cost of £12,000. Hope Waddell Training Institution remained one of the most outstanding mission institutions as the government report of 1907 shows. The report states:

> The Bonny Government School, the Benin City Government School, the Hope Waddell Institute (Scottish Free Church Mission) and other large and more advanced schools are doing excellent work in training teachers. (Nwabara, 1977, p. 62)

The report of the Education Department of 1905 described Hope Waddell as "the largest secondary school in the colony."

The Catholic Mission

The Roman Catholic missionary work in Nigeria fell within the spheres of two Catholic evangelical societies, the Society for African Missions, founded by Father de Bressilac in 1856, and the Holy Ghost Fathers founded in Paris in 1841. By an official arrangement, the Society for African Missions was responsible for evangelization work between Rivers Volta and the Niger while the Holy Ghost Fathers were assigned to the area between Rivers Niger to the east and the Congo. Thus, while Yorubaland fell within the sphere of work of the Society for African Missions, the area east of the Niger fell within the sphere of influence of the Holy Ghost Fathers.

The Vicariate of the Bight of Benin

The area between Rivers Volta and the Niger which was under the sphere of influence of the Society for African Missions was called the Vicariate of the Bight of Benin. Rev. Father Broghero, an Italian, of the Society for African Missions came to Lagos from Dahomey on February 17, 1862. In 1868 a mission was created for Lagos with Father Pierre Bouche as the first parish priest under Vicar Apostolic Father Broghero. Father Pierre Bouche built a chapel and in 1869, a school was started in Lagos by two Irish brothers. In 1876, the Roman Catholics started an experimental farm near Badagry on a ten-mile piece of land which they had acquired through the help of Sir James Marshall. As natives cleared the land for the mission, they were given personal parcels of land in return for their services. This agricultural estate was called Topo. Indeed, within a few years there existed a large population of native inhabitants on this estate and they were encouraged by the mission to remain there permanently as a separate Christian community where they could teach monogamy and discourage fetish practices. Another reason for the establishment of the plantation estate was to give functional education to their pupils. In other words, they wanted the products of their schools to be self-sufficient and self-employed rather than hanker after clerical work in government offices which in most instances was not forthcoming. In 1892, the Catholic mission established a convent school for girls at Topo. In spite of the seeming failure of the Christian mission experimental farms, about three-quarters of the pupils who received any form of industrial education in Lagos were products of Catholic institutions in Topo and at St. Mary's convent school. In 1876, the St. Gregory's College was founded in Lagos which combined teacher training with grammar school instruction.

The educational work of the Society for African Missions was further enhanced when four sisters of the congregation of the Franciscan Sisters of the Propagation of the Faith arrived in Lagos from Lyons in 1872. Two other members of the same congregation arrived in 1874. These women served in different capacities both in the schools and the dispensaries. The most spectacular among them were Sister Colette (d. 1916) and Sister Veronique (d. 1942) who worked very consistently toward the development of education and medical services in Nigeria.

The Response to Missionary Education in Southern Nigeria

The work of missionaries was not easy sailing even in Southern Nigeria, for while a few Africans and their rulers patronized missionary enterprise, others rejected missionary intrusion in any form. On the whole, support or lack of support for missionary work was greatly influenced by internal developments in Southern Nigeria. In Yorubaland, for instance, the Egbas, under their ruler Sodeke, accepted missionaries because they expected military help from the British government against their enemies. King Manuwa of Ijebuland patronized missionaries because he wanted his town to become a trading entrepot for the Ijesha, Ondo, and Ekiti districts. Kurumi, the ruler of Ijaye, patronized missionaries because he thought that the settlement of missionaries in his midst would enhance his prestige and attract traders to his territory. The Efik people of Calabar patronized missionaries because they wanted agricultural development and instruction in methods of making sugar.

When the chiefs of Bonny wrote asking for missionaries in 1848 they insisted on those who would be capable of teaching their young people the English language (Ayandele, 1969, pp. 28-29; Berman, 1975, pp. 24-25).

Except for these pockets of acceptance, missionaries were neither accepted nor tolerated in most parts of Southern Nigeria. Consequently, missionaries turned their attention to youths and schools as sources of conversion because they soon realized, to their utter dismay and puzzlement, the futility of trying to convert men of good standing in Nigerian society. Indeed, as one Roman Catholic missionary lamented:

> For a man of social status to accept Christianity in this country...is to expose himself to poverty for the rest of his life; it is to renounce, as the Lord asks of the Religious only, his fortune, his future and even his family. (Ekechi, 1972, p. 176)

Hence, as Ekechi claims, "formal education became the bait with which the young generation was enticed to Christianity" (p. 176). Good education, it was believed, would enable young African men to earn a good living as well as exert their own influence and that of their adopted religious denomination upon the society at large.

The Development of Western Education in Northern Nigeria

The development of Western education between the south and north of Nigeria progressed differently because before the advent of Western education into Southern Nigeria pioneered by Christian missionaries, Northern Nigeria had had centuries of Islamic scholarship (Ayandele, 1967, p. 117; Gbadamosi, 1967, p. 89; Fafunwa, 1974, p. 100; Solaru, 1964, p. 19).

The first attempt by Christian missions to establish in Northern Nigeria was during the Niger expedition of 1841 which included, among others, Rev. (later Bishop) Samuel Ajayi Crowther. When the expedition reached Lokoja, a model farm was established there but the project was unfortunately abandoned thereafter. In July 1857, Rev. Samuel Ajayi Crowther and others undertook another expedition up the Niger. Crowther was given land to build a mission house at Idah and Gbebe but the whole project crumbled when their ship, the Dayspring, was shipwrecked at Jebba.

However, in 1865, Dr. Baikie of the CMS founded a settlement at Lokoja and opened a school there in the same year where instructions were given in Hausa and Nupe languages (Fafunwa 1974, p. 101). Reports also have it that a Catholic school was opened at Lokoja in 1869 (Gbadamosi, 1967, p. 93).

It was the burning desire of the Christian missions to win for the cross the souls of those Northern Nigerians whom they described as "followers of the false prophet." It was also their desire to establish schools for the development of the minds of their new converts. Accordingly, as early as 1855, T. J. Bowen of the Southern Baptist Mission of America tried to establish a station in the very populous Muslim city of Ilorin. Through his personal friendship with the Emirs of Nupe, Bishop Crowther established stations at Lokoja, Egga and Kipo Hill. By 1880, the Wesleyan Missionary Society and the Church Missionary Society were eager to establish stations as far north as Chad. And the year before, W. Allakurah Sharpe, a Wesleyan agent of Kanuri descent, had appealed to his Society for help to establish the gospel among his people in Bornu. Indeed, by the 1890s, the American Baptist missionaries had proposed to vacate all white missionaries from the south to the north despite the fact that the Sudan Party led by Graham Wilmot Brooke and eleven graduates from Oxford and Cambridge met with unparalleled failure in 1890 in Northern Nigeria. However, in 1899 the Toronto Industrial Mission Missionaries were allowed to occupy Pategi, a Muslim town on the Niger. In 1902, the same missionaries were allowed into Bida with the full cooperation of the Resident and the Emir.

The Roman Catholic Holy Ghost Fathers made relentless efforts to open stations at Ibi and Bassa in 1902, and were forced to withdraw from the northern missionary field in 1905 after several unsuccessful attempts. In 1904, the CMS were allowed to open in Zaria City. In that same year, the Cambridge University Mission Party, later known as the Sudan United Mission, began work at Wase. In 1905, the Mennonite Brethren of the USA opened a station at Ilorin. In the same year the CMS were invited to open stations at Kontagora and Katsina. In 1905, too, Lord Lugard granted permission to the CMS to open in Kano.

Having been given permission to open various stations in the north, the CMS geared its efforts toward educational work. In 1903, a British schoolmaster was appointed to take charge of the Lokoja school with a Nigerian as his assistant. The Sudan Interior Mission opened farms at Pategi, Wushishi and Bida. The CMS opened a school for mallams in Bida in the hope of teaching court officials to write Nupe and Hausa languages in English scripts. Two West Indian teachers were employed to teach in the school which ran from 7 am to 9 am. Though the school was to be secular, the subjects included the scriptures, geography, singing, reading, writing the vernacular, the New Testament and Bible stories. English language was added to the curriculum later on. In 1907, Dr. Walter Miller of the CMS established two schools in Zaria, one for educating the mallams and the other for the education of the chief's sons. In a different development, Resident Mayor of Sokoto, Burdon started an unofficial school in Sokoto in 1909. In the same year Resident H. R. Palmer opened a school at Katsina. These schools supplemented the efforts of the Quranic schools whose enrollment stood at 218,618 pupils in 1914 (Fafunwa, 1974, p. 100).

It is important to make the point that the early Christian mission schools in Northern Nigeria failed to thrive because the missions were bent on using the schools as means of conversion. Indeed, one CMS Secretary made the point very clearly when he wrote:

> ...we shall use the gospel as our textbook and carefully chosen text as writing copies, I feel it will be very definitely a missionary opportunity. Also, if people see these mallams coming to us for teaching we shall possibly later on be able to open a school on more definite missionary lines. (Fafunwa, 1974, p. 103)

Indeed, even while Walter Miller was willing to run his two schools along secular lines, he made it absolutely clear that he must be:

> left perfectly free to give them whatever positive religious

> instructions I like... They would attend the usual morning and evening prayers with all the rest of the household and beyond that is the atmosphere which is bound to pervade a house *where the life and teaching and love of Christ are paramount*; my aim will be so to permeate these boys with a sense of justice, righteousness, truth, purity, cleanliness and manliness (none of which they have!) that another day, even though not while at school, they will think of these things in connection with those they knew as Christians... (Fafunwa, 1974, p. 105)

Besides, the chiefs and Emirs in the north were unwilling to send their children to school and the students on their part were skeptical of Western education in and of itself.

What was Britain's attitude towards the Christian churches and by implication Western education in Northern Nigeria? Britain's attitude towards the church and Western education was summed up in a speech Lord Lugard, the British High Commissioner in Northern Nigeria, gave at the installation of the new Sultan of Sokoto in 1903, for, in a country where the school was an "adjunct of the Church" (Fafunwa, 1974, p. 81), what affected the church affected the schools as well. In his speech of 1903, Lord Lugard outlined what was to be the guiding principles of British policy on religion in Northern Nigeria in later years as follows; "Government will in no way interfere with religion. All men are free to worship God as they please. Mosques and prayer places will be treated with respect by us..." (Gbadamosi, 1967, p 94).

In this proclamation, Lord Lugard promised not only freedom of worship but respect for Islam in Nigeria. Consequently, Christian missionaries were not allowed into emirates of Northern Nigeria except with the expressed permission of the Emirs. However, even when they were allowed to open stations in some parts of the north the work of the Christian missions and indeed Western education in Northern Nigeria was a dismal failure largely because Lugard's successors adhered strictly, if not more so, to Lugard's enunciation of 1903. Sir Percy Girouard, Lugard's immediate successor, even revoked the permission given to the CMS to establish in certain townships in the north because he did not want the "Christian missions to spoil the Northerners as they had done the Southerners" (Ayandele, 1967, p. 146). Little wonder then, that when Girouard wrote to Lord Lugard in Hong Kong in 1908, he said:

> Personally I should like to see the Missions withdraw entirely from the Northern States, for the best missionary for the present will be the high-minded, clean living British Resident. (Ayandele, 1967, p. 147)

Another point is that both Lugard and his successors were contemptuous and scornful of educated Africans. Of educated Africans, Lugard once wrote:

> I am somewhat baffled as to how to get in touch with the Educated Native... I am not in sympathy with him. His loud and arrogant conceit are distasteful to me, his lack of natural dignity and courtesy antagonize me. (Perham, 1960, p. 586)

And to Sir Girouard, Christian education produced "a denationalized and disorganized" people (Gbadamosi, 1967, p. 95). The colonial administrators also restricted the movement of missionaries because they believed that they were capable of spying on government officials and on some of the corrupt Emirs in the north. Of greater concern to the British administrators, however, was the instability of their newly acquired territory the administration of which required tranquility in view of the scarce resources at their disposal, inadequate military personnel, staff and poor communication network. The British officials were therefore unwilling to risk confrontation of any sort which could lead to civil uprisings. More so, by the time of the introduction of Christianity into Southern Nigeria, Northern Nigeria had had centuries of Islamic education. It must be noted that Islam was not only a religion but also a way of life. Any imposition therefore was capable of causing a jihad. "The natural suspicions and dislike with which the first Christian government was first regarded by the Moslem," maintained Lugard, "rendered it inadvisable even if it had been possible to embark on any educational efforts at first" (Gbadamosi, 1967, p. 97). During a visit to Northern Nigeria in 1906, Dr. A. V. Murray perceived the possibility of a jihad in the event of any imposition on the Muslims and wrote:

> I was assured by men who otherwise showed a keen sense of humor that the Muslim emirs were sullen and suspicious and that to attempt to allow the missions to introduce modern schools on Christian lines...might cause a jehad (sic) to blow up at once. (Gbadamosi, 1967, p. 97)

These factors therefore, forced the colonial government to take direct responsibility for education in Northern Nigeria. Earlier in 1905, Lord Lugard had sketched the four stages of educational development he had envisioned for the north which included first - a Mallam's school, where in addition to the 3Rs, Geography and Hausa would be taught; second - a school for the sons of chiefs and Emirs designed to produce a "generation of loyal and enlightened rulers without necessarily foregoing their religion"; third - the ordinary primary school of a secular nature; fourth - "cantonment schools," designed to produce native clerks (see Gbadamosi 1967, p. 99 fn). Consistent with his belief that it was "advisable to educate Mohammedans along their own lines and (that) compulsory attendance at a Christian school is inconceivable and might prove disastrous", Girouard, and in short, the government established the Nassarawa Central Schools in Kano in 1910 based on Islamic lines as envisioned by Lord Lugard in 1905. Before the schools were established, it must be pointed out, Dr. Hans Vischer who had become the Director of Education in the Northern Provinces in 1908, was sponsored by the government to undertake a tour of the Gold Coast (now Ghana), Egypt, the Sudan and Lagos to see first-hand how Western Education was run along Muslim lines in these countries and places.

The opening of the Nassarawa schools marked a turning point in the educational development of the north. On this Mr. H. H. Bell, the Governor of that region, wrote in 1911:

> An important commencement has been made toward the education of natives by the establishment of the school at Kano, which it is hoped may ultimately be organized on the lines of the Gordon College, Khartoum...more than a hundred Mallams (Mohammedan priests) are now under instruction and learning the rudiments of History and

Geography, Arithmetic and Simple Sciences. These men will become teachers in native schools all over the protectorate and will disseminate such knowledge as is appropriate to the present condition of the population. (Solaru, 1964, p. 20)

The Nassarawa schools were organized in four stages. The mallam's school admitted mallams ranging from ages 18 to 30 who were seconded to it from the provincial headquarters of the north. The mallams were given lessons sufficient to enable them to manage new schools. There was the school for the sons of chiefs and Emirs. They were taught the 3Rs to enable them to take advantage of positions in the new Native Administration. There was the technical or craft school designed for the sons of the servants of the Emirs. Students in this school were taught to be carpenters, blacksmiths, leather workers, and weavers. Finally, there was the usual primary school designed to produce clerks for the expanding civil services in the north. In every case, however, students were required to attend Quranic schools. To support their religious practices, the government constructed a mosque near the schools at its own expense (Gbadamosi, 1967, p. 99). All the schools emphasized technical, industrial and agricultural education as well as classical learning for Muslim teachers and the use of the vernacular.

By 1913, the Nassarawa schools had 209 pupils on its roll, distributed as follows:

Table 1

Statistics of Pupils in Nassarawa Schools, 1913

Province	No. Of Pupils	Province	No. Of Pupils
Kano	59	Nassarawa	12
Niger	40	Yola	11
Muri	25	Zaria	7
Bornu	17	Ilorin	6
Central	13	Sokoto	6
Kontagora	13		

Source: Fafunwa, 1974, p. 108

In May 1914, the Nassarawa schools were closed down and were replaced by Provincial schools which were primary schools with teacher training wings attached to those at Sokoto, Gwandu, Kebbi, Bida, Zaria and Katsina (Gbadamosi, 1967, p. 100). Their pupils were drawn predominantly from the ruling class and their course of studies lasted for five years. Their curriculum consisted of the 3Rs in addition to History, Geography and English. For the first two years, teaching was in Hausa. English was introduced in the third, fourth and fifth years. This remained the pattern of educational development in Northern Nigeria to about 1926. Of particular significance in this development was the Sokoto Provincial school which had a craft center attached to it. Also notable was the Kano school which had a craft center that produced such scarce commodities as carts, furniture, office equipment, shoes and at times motor parts. Though secular in tone, these schools included the teaching of Hausa, Arabic and Islamic studies in their curriculum, for it was their duty, as Sir Hugh Clifford maintained, "to teach those boys not only the lessons learned from books which they will here acquire, but the way that good Muhammedans should live, the good behaviour and courteous deportment without which mere book learning is of little worth" (Gbadamosi, 1967, p. 100). Local leaders were co-opted into the school boards. For instance, their governing councils consisted of local chiefs and other prominent men from the locality. This measure, more than any other, provided a major attraction to the public schools. Hence, average attendance rose from 100 in 1910 to 320 by December 1911 and from 354 in 1914 to 750 by 1916 (Solaru, 1964, p. 21; Gbadamosi, 1967, p. 101). And according to Gbadamosi (1967):

> By 1919, there were 21 Government schools in use with one nearing completion and six more under construction. By 1923, the total number of Government schools had risen to 39 with a total enrollment of 1,955 boys. Out of these 39 schools, two were in Bornu, four in Sokoto, five in Zaria and eight in Kano. By 1926, the number of Government schools shot up to 69 with a total enrollment of 2,454 pupils. In this year, Bornu Province had seven Government schools, Kano five, Zaria six and Sokoto fourteen. (p. 101)

Another milestone was reached in educational development in Northern Nigeria when Sir Hugh Clifford opened the Katsina Teacher's Training College in 1922. It was a five-year institution which Sir Clifford described as a school for training "young Muhammedan men of birth and standing from all the Muslim Emirates in Nigeria," as teachers (Gbadamosi, 1967, p. 100). He further pointed out that it would be the duty of the products of Katsina College:

> to teach those boys (their pupils) not only the lessons learned from books which they will here acquire, but the way that good Muhammedans should live, the good manners, good behaviour and courteous deportment without which mere book learning is of little worth. (Gbadamosi, 1967, p. 100)

Despite the above statistics, the acceptance of Western education in Northern Nigeria remained a far cry compared to its population. Government played the dominant role in education. Islamic education continued to be popular with the people as the census figures of 1921 in Table 2 show.

The acceptance of Western education in whatever form was a very modest one indeed in Northern Nigeria, for up to 1921 only .48% of the population was educated (Meek, 1969, p. 254).

Table 2

Education Statistics for Northern Nigeria, 1921

All provinces and townships

Religion or denomination	Schools	Scholars	Teachers
Church Missionary Society	58	1,658	82
Dutch Reformed Church	2	57	5
Mennonite Brethren in Christ	3	95	5
Nigerian Pastorate Church	2	225	2
Roman Catholic Mission	5	350	10
Seventh Day Adventists	1	32	3
Sudan Interior Mission	18	225	22
Sudan United Mission	13	247	31
United African Church	1	75	2
All Christian Denominations	103	2,964	162
Muslim	30,411	63,370	35,093
Grand Total	30,514	166,344	32,255
Percentage of Christian	0.34	1.8	0.46
Percentage of Muslim	99.66	98.2	99.54

Source: Meek, 1969, p. 263

What were the reasons for the apparent reluctance of the North to take advantage of Western education? The reasons were many and varied. In the first place, Muslims were suspicious of Christian content in the curriculum of even the government schools. This suspicion was heightened by the association of Dr. Hans Vischer, a former missionary, with the Nassarawa schools. Tradition also played a part in the reluctance of northerners to accept Western education. Northern Nigeria, it must be observed, was not subject to external influences like Egypt, Syria and Turkey. Hence, while other Muslim countries were synthesizing the old and the new, Northern Nigeria continued in its conservative path. Besides, Northern Nigeria was shielded from the Christian and modernizing influences from the south of Nigeria. However, of demonstrable significance was the fact that Muslim education still had relevance in the north under the indirect rule system. It was the education which produced "...judges, administrators and religious men who sustained the administration and maintained the tone of religious life in the Muslim North" (Gbadamosi, 1967, p. 102). Also significant was the fact that the Emirs lacked any firm commitment to the pursuit of Western education itself. Hence, they never challenged the British authorities on educational matters. For example, throughout the British rule in Northern Nigeria, no Emir ever requested more money for educational purposes in his emirate (Ozigi & Ocho, 1981, p. 41). It is believed that the Emirs feared the emerging class of educated mallams as possible threats to their religious and political authority. It is also argued that the Emirs refused to send their promising sons to school therefore undermining the value and prestige of education. Finally, it is believed that given the conservative nature of Northern Nigerian society, changes which follow the introduction of Western education were seen not only as unnecessary but as dangerous.

Tibenderana (1983, 1985) has added a different dimension to the educational backwardness of the north controversy. He argues that the blame often leveled at Emirs as the main contributory factors in the educational underdevelopment of Northern Nigeria is misleading and erroneous because it is based on a misconception that, under the indirect rule system, the Emirs preserved and even increased their power and authority. But contrary to this misconception, the real rulers in Northern Nigeria were the British with Emirs serving as mere assistants: the sovereignty of the Emirs having been taken away from them in their letters of appointment which in every case without exception warned the Emirs not to appoint officials without the consent of the Government except on judicial matters. The Emirs were required to obey all orders from the Governor and "in all other matters in the Goverment of the land, it is your duty to follow the orders of the Resident..." (Tibenderana, 1983, p. 519). The Emirs could neither raise taxes nor authorize expenditure without the permission of the Governor, and were threatened with sanctions if they failed to comply with all the rules. Even the power to spend native administration money was vested in the Resident who in turn received his authority from the Lieutenant-Governor. To support this connection, Tibenderana (1983) cites the example of the Sultan of Sokoto who was denied permission to spend a meagre sum of £69 (sixty-nine pounds) in 1917 for the construction of a dormitory to house pupils who lived far away from school and who had nowhere to stay in town. This proposal was rejected even though it had the blessings of E. J. Arnett, the Resident. "If the Sultan of Sokoto, a first class chief, could not expend a meagre sum of £69 of his native administration's revenue without the approval of the Lieutenant-Governor," Tibenderana wonders, "who of the other emirs would do so?" The truth of the matter is that the Emirs had no power over their revenue and could not draw up budgets, which made it impossible for them to initiate educational projects. Tibenderana concludes that the "...role of the emirs in the expenditure of native administration revenue was that of onlookers who waited patiently to be given some assignment to carry out by their British masters" (1983, p. 520). On the other hand, he argues that the Emirs contributed positively and immensely to the spread of Western education in Northern Nigeria by "their early appreciation of its political and social significance, when it was first introduced in the emirates, during the second decade of this century" (Tibenderana, 1983, p. 520). Consequently, they did not have to wait or be compelled to send their children to the newly established native administration schools because they had come to terms with the fact that their children could not hope to succeed them without formal education under the colonial situation. It was for this reason, Tibenderana maintains,

> that the majority of the emirs clamoured to have their sons and brothers admitted to native administration schools and to Kaduna College which until 1948 was the only secondary school in Northern Nigeria. (Tibenderana, 1983, p. 521)

It was therefore no accident that ten brothers of the Emir of Gwandu and two of his nephews were attending Birnin Kebbi elementary school by 1920. Indeed, two other brothers of the same Emir were receiving private tuition in the 3Rs because they were considered too old to attend a regular primary school. To support this contention, Tibenderana (1983), cites the following statistics which I find interesting enough to reproduce here:

> All the First Class Chiefs of Sultan Abubakar's generation, namely Ahmed, the Lamido of Adamawa (1943-53), Samaila, the emir of Argungu (1942-53), Yahaya, the emir of Gwandu (1938-57), Usman Nagogo, the emir of Katsina (1944-81) and Ja'afaru, the emir of Zaria (1937-59), received formal Western education. The other five First Class Chiefs-namely Umar Ibu Muhammad Al Amin Al Kenemi, the Shehu of Bornu; Yakubu, the emir of Bauchi; Abdulkadir, the emir of Ilorin; Abdullah Bayero, the emir of Kano and Muhammad Ndayako, the emir of Bida, who in 1952 were aged eighty, sixty-three, sixty-five, seventy-six and seventy respectively - were too old to attend school when native administration schools were established in their emirates during the second decade of this century (p.521)

Tibenderana maintains that it is also not true to say that the Emirs refused to send their children to school for fear of being converted to Christianity or because they did not realize the importance of Western education. What is true is that the Emirs did not want their children to undertake long and hazardous journeys to Kano for the purpose of education since at this time the most readily available means of transportation was on horseback or by trekking. Accordingly, when the British agreed to establish primary schools in all the provincial headquarters, the Emirs quickly took advantage of it to educate their sons and wards. Hence, by 1925, of all the pupils attending Bida primary school, 67% of them were sons of native administration officials. Indeed, not only did the Emirs send their own children to school, they encouraged their subordinates to do so too. Thus, by 1930, more than 60% of the pupils in Sokoto province were sons of native administration officials and the Emirs. And before 1930, more than 80% of all those who entered Katsina College were sons of Emirs and native administration workers (Tibenderana, 1983)..

Tibenderana (1983) further argues that there is sufficient evidence on record to confirm that the Emirs not only patronized education for their sons and wards but encouraged the education of the sons of commoners (talakawas) as well. To support his contention, he argued that in 1938-39, for example, many Emirs objected to the establishment of a princes' middle school for their children despite British pressure and the imminent benefits such a school would confer on their own children. Arguing against the establishment of the school, Abdullah Kadiri, the Emir of Ilorin, maintained that the Emir's sons would receive the best education if they were educated together with the children of commoners. This objection was upheld by the Emirs of Adamawa, Argungu, Katsina and Zaria. In another development Samaila, the Emir of Argungu, in an address to the conference of Chiefs in 1943 appealed to the British colonial authorities to allow them to institute free meals for the sons of commoners because this would:

> ...mitigate the sufferings of the Talakawa's sons who ...frequently arrived at school in the morning insufficiently fed, making it impossible for them to concentrate on their studies - whereas if a free meal was provided, they would perform better in their examinations, thus making the educational system more efficient. (Tibenderana 1983, p. 524)

This act of kindness, the Emirs reasoned, would enhance the cause of Western education among commoners. The proposal was unanimously accepted by the conference but due to lack of funds, each local administration was required to implement the decision within the limits of its finances. According to Tibenderana

(1983), the real clog in the wheels of progress in the development of Western education in Northern Nigeria were the British whose policies,

> were adverse to missionary enterprise, including education, especially in the Muslim emirates because they wanted to maintain the status quo and to avoid the production of 'disgruntled intellectuals' who were held culpable for anti-British activities in such places as India, Egypt and Lagos. (p. 525)

Hence, the British officials clamped down on missionary activities in Northern Nigeria, in the hope that by so doing, they would maintain "a turbulence-free and cheap administration which in turn would prolong the era of Pax Britannica in Northern Nigeria" (Tibenderana, 1983, p. 525). Indeed, there was the distinct case of the Maguzawa who wanted to have missionaries in their midst in 1912 but were denied permission because the British officials believed that Christian teachings will make the Maguzawa disloyal to Muslim authorities and that missionaries will not withstand the temptation of not preaching to Muslims (Ayandele, 1966, p. 149). For reasons already given, therefore, the British officials were generally reluctant to grant permission for missionary enterprise in Northern Nigeria in the pretext that the Emirs were opposed to missionaries and missionary enterprise. Indeed, Tibenderana's contention is supported by Article 13e of the Education Ordinance of 1916 which stated that:

> no grant shall be made to any school or training institution which is a Mission or other Christian School or training institution situated in a District of the Northern Provinces in which no Mission or other Christian school or training institution is established at the commencement of the Ordinance. (Callaway, 1987, p. 136)

Like Ayandele[10] (1967) before him, Tibenderana (1983) maintains that the Emirs, wherever they did so, were opposed to missionary enterprise mainly for political reasons, for, according to him,

> ...missionaries particularly the British ones, viewed their role in Northern Nigeria not only as that of spreading the gospel but of defending the political rights of the Hausa peasantry against Fulani misrule and oppression. (p. 526)

True to Tibenderana's contention, evidence abounds in the research literature of anti-Fulani sentiments being fanned by missionaries. For example, by 1891, the Hausa Association formed for the study of Hausa language was already calling on Britain to destroy the Fulani impostors so that the thirst of the Hausa for Christianity might be achieved (Ayandele, 1967, p. 124). In another development, the CMS hailed the British expeditions against Ilorin and Bida because:

> the Hausa race which was being mulcted by the Fulani impostors..., would soon be liberated and slavery given a mortal blow...Fulah (sic) oppression is now to be superseded by the direct exercise of British authority. (Ayandele, 1967, p. 126)

In a letter to F. Baylis, the CMS Secretary, Dr. Walter Miller, contended that; "the slavery of Socoto (sic) and raiding in all the 7 big Hausa states is terrible and will have to be put down" (Ayandele, 1967, p. 127). Then again in 1900, Miller wrote in his Niger and Yoruba notes:

> The end is drawing near. The kings of Hausa cities are renouncing their religious allegiance to the Sultan of Sokoto. The people prophesy the advent of the whiteman with the Christian religion, which all the world will accept for a short space of forty months... The sacred writings of the Hausas predict the second coming of Christ as the victorious leader of a great army. Next year (1900) is marked out as the time. So it comes to pass that the whole Hausa world is waiting for Christ. Now, we believe that Christ will appear in Hausaland next year, not as the people expect Him however. He will appear, not as a true Moslem, the son of a false faith, but as the crucified one, the Son of God. (Ayandele, 1967, p. 128)

Indeed as late as 1920, the Diocesan Synod of Lagos maintained that:

> ...the presence of enlightened and Christian people in such Muslim states may do much to bring to light the abuses and oppressions incidental to indirect rule through Muslim chiefs (Ubah, 1976, p.366)

In another but related development, Tibenderana (1983, 1985) blames the British administration for the tardy development of girls' education in Northern Nigeria. According to him, the British administration did not contemplate the establishment of a girls' school in Northern Nigeria until 1929, that is, nineteen years after similar schools had been established for boys in the north. He points out that it was only in 1929 that E. R. J. Hussey, the first Director of Education in Nigeria, proposed the establishment of two girls' centers at Kano and Katsina. This suggestion was most welcomed by the Emirs of Kano and Katsina, Muhammad Bayero and Muhammad Dikko respectively. After the establishment of the two institutions at Kano and Katsina, other Emirs, namely, the Sultan of Sokoto Hassan, and Usman the Emir of Gwandu appealed to Mr. G. J. Lethem, the Acting Lieutenant-Governor of the Northern provinces in 1933 for the establishment of similar institutions in their capitals as well. Again, in May of the same year, the two Emirs reiterated their appeal to Lethem in an interview with him at Kaduna. At this point, Mr. Lethem was convinced of the Emirs' desire for a girls' institution and accordingly discussed the matter with E. R. J. Hussey, the Director of Education, despite his earlier objection to the scheme due to lack of funds and personnel. Mr. Hussey discussed the matter with the two Emirs during their official visit to Lagos in June 1933. On that occasion, Mr. Hussey made it clear to the Emirs that, apart from financial constraints, the government would find it difficult to recruit the two European women teachers needed to start the school following the pattern in Kano and Katsina. To make the Director's work easier, the Emirs agreed to accept Yoruba women as teachers instead and promised to pay their salaries. In 1934, therefore, two additional girls' schools were established at Sokoto and near Birnin Kebbi. Following on the footsteps of Usman and Hassan, the Emirs of Argungu, Bornu, Ilorin and Zaria demanded girls' schools for their emirates as well. Unfortunately, their demands were never met due to financial constraints. And in 1935, the British administration decided on co-education instead of establishing purely girls' schools. The Emirs were staunchly opposed to this scheme because they foresaw that their subjects would be unwilling to patronize co-education because, it was thought, co-education would breed promiscuity among female students. True to the Emirs' fears, enrollments of girls in the co-educational schools dropped drastically. In 1947, for example, 314 girls were enrolled in schools in Sokoto province where girls were taught in separate classrooms, whereas during the same year the number of girls enrolled in Kano, Niger, Ilorin and Bornu where girls were taught in the same classrooms as boys dropped drastically (Tibenderana, 1983, p. 530). During the same year, native administration girls' schools at Kano, Katsina, Birnin Kebbi and Sokoto were running at their full capacity of 300 students.

Also important in the educational underdevelopment of the north controversy, is the fact that requests for more elementary schools by Northern Emirs were not heeded by the British administration. In 1934, for instance, Sule, the Emir of Fika's request for more elementary schools and a middle school in his emirate was not granted despite the Emir's explanation that, given the prevailing circumstances, it was impossible for a boy to advance beyond elementary school in his emirate. Even the Emir's request for the extension of the number of years in primary school in the absence of a middle school was also rejected. The refusal to establish a middle school at Fika stemmed from the British policy of establishing only one middle school in a particular emirate. This policy was responsible for the closure of the Birnin Kebbi middle school in 1935, because there already existed a middle school in Sokoto emirate.

The point must also be made that as early as 1917 the Emirs were protesting the non-inclusion of the English language in the primary school curriculum in the north despite the fact that for many years English was already a part of the primary school curriculum in the south. Indeed, it was not until 1948 that the English language was included in the primary school curriculum in the north after a series of vehement protests from northern Emirs.

I wish to state that Tibenderana's (1983) contention that during the indirect rule system in Northern Nigeria, the Emirs were "British assistants and not rulers" is persuasive but not convincing, for if anything, evidence suggests that the Emirs were still masters in their own houses. This view is exemplified by the series of hostile encounters between the Emirs on the one hand and the white missionaries on the other which in every case the Emirs came out victorious. Ayandele (1967) describes one such encounter in Kano and states:

> The missionaries were very fortunate to escape being murdered... In fact, perhaps never in their lives were they so near to death as they were when they arrived in Kano. There was a heated discussion for over three hours between the Emir, Aliyu 'the Great', and about forty of his lieutenants. The Emir was rather inclined to kill the missionaries, as the majority of the chiefs wished. But the Waziri put his foot down that the missionaries should not be molested. What made wiser counsel prevail in the Emir's court was the military subjugation of Zinder, a neighbouring town, by the French after the killing there of two Frenchmen. If the Kanawa killed the missionaries, the argument went, they would suffer the same fate. (p. 135)

Another incident to emphasize here was in 1927 involving Dr. Walter Miller of the CMS and the Emir of Zaria which required the personal intervention of the Governor-General of Nigeria himself. The crisis came to a head when, in 1927, Dr. Miller of the CMS constructed a new church in Zaria without the authority of the Emir or the Resident. When the Emir learned that the building was for Christian worship, he ordered that a seven-foot wall be constructed to cut it off from public view and enclose it within Miller's compound. In the settlement that followed the Governor-General of Nigeria's intervention, the CMS was compelled to find a new site for its operations at Wusasa outside Zaria city.

Tibenderana's contention that it was not true to say that the Emirs refused to send their children to school for fear of being converted to Christianity is not supported by evidence either. Indeed, Fafunwa (1974) maintains that:

> Since missionary schools were established primarily to convert children and young adults to the Christian faith, the Muslims in the north and south saw this as a definite threat to their own faith. The schools in those days (and even today) were places where pupils went in as pagans and Muslims, and came out as converted Christians. To prevent the wholesale conversion of Muslims to Christianity, the Muslims, particularly the Emirs and other leaders in the south, refused to send their children to Christian schools.(p. 100)

As Tibenderana has aptly demonstrated in his research, the Emirs were interested in the education of their sons and relatives for its "political and social significance" because they had come to realize that "under a colonial situation, their scions could not hope to continue to hold on to the reins of power unless they acquired the white man's education" (p. 520). Although in a few instances, the Emirs showed some interest in the education of the children of commoners, these were acts of tokenism which came often too late to make any lasting impression on the large downtrodden poor population of the north.

Finally, Ubah's (1976) assertion that the Emirs, as political and religious leaders of their people, were required by Muslim law to protect the religion, for not to do so would be apostasy -- a great sin, must be taken seriously. Explaining this contention he states:

> ...one of the most important justifications for the existence of the emirate (or imamate) was the safeguarding of the religion... Each emir was the defensor fidei within the area of authority. He could not willingly welcome the missionaries and by so doing sponsor proselytization...(Hence) the emirs could not of their own volition let in the missionaries with-out abdicating their solemn responsibilities as Muslim rulers, without antagonizing their subjects and in particular, the Muslim intelligentsia.[11] (Ubah, 1976, pp. 352, 353, 354).

Given the above scenario, therefore, it is safe to say that the blame for the educational underdevelopment of Northern Nigeria must be shared between the Emirs, the British administration and the people themselves. Anything less will not do justice.

CHAPTER IV

MISSIONARY RIVALRY AND EDUCATIONAL EXPANSION IN NIGERIA 1885-1945

Evidence abounds in the research literature to show that wherever the Protestant and Catholic missionaries met in Africa, opposition, antagonism, and rivalry flared between them. For instance, the Lutherans were expelled from Abyssinia (now Ethiopia) in 1832 because of Jesuit intrigues. The Jesuits also frustrated the efforts of Johann Krapf (a Lutheran missionary in Abyssinia) and his work among the Gallas in the Kingdom of Shoa in 1844. A. M. Mackay's attempt to spread the gospel among the Ugandans was similarly foiled by Roman Catholic missionaries (Naylor, 1905, pp. 132-133; Oliver, 1967, pp. 5, 6, 67, 74). In Buganda, a French Catholic missionary order called the White Fathers effectively challenged the Anglicans and spread their own brand of evangelical and educational work throughout east and central Africa (Berman, 1975, pp. 12, 21; Oliver, 1967, p. 74; Bassey, 1991).

In Nigeria, however, missionary rivalry was even more intense. Apart from theological differences, nationality factors came into play. While most of the Protestant missionaries in Nigeria came from England and Scotland, most of the Catholic missionaries came from either France or Ireland. Indeed, France was Britain's greatest rival for colonies in Africa in the 19th century, and Ireland was (and remains to this day) Britain's unruly colony. According to Abernethy (1969):

> Intense rivalry began in (Nigeria) during the early years of this century. As both Catholics and Anglicans spread out from their common headquarters,...they quickly became engaged in leapfrogging operations. (p. 46)

The year 1885 marks the beginning of the missionary scramble for the souls of Nigerians. After the Berlin Conference of 1884-1885, European nations were required to show evidence of effective occupation for any territory to which they laid claims. Accordingly, soldiers, traders, merchants, and missionaries alike were sent afield and used by the various imperial governments to satisfy this clause of the treaty. The result of this scramble was the establishment of unprecedented numbers of schools by the various religious organizations particularly in Southern Nigeria. The schools, unfortunately, became important avenues for proselytization (Bassey, 1991).

The School Revolution in Nigeria

The period between 1885 and 1945 witnessed intense missionary rivalry in Nigeria occasioned by the entry of the Holy Ghost Fathers into the missionary field in Eastern Nigeria. Competition between the various missions in Nigeria led to what could be called an education revolution in Southern Nigeria because missionaries in attempting to convert the youths turned their attention to schools. And as Father Lejeune wrote, "without schools we would be nothing."

It should be pointed out that although the Roman Catholics were the greatest exponents of the "evangelization through the school" policy, they were not its only beneficiary, for when Mr. and Mrs. de Graft of the Wesleyan Methodist Mission opened their first school in Badagry, Nigeria in 1843, they called it the "Nursery of the Infant Church", meaning that the school was to be a breeding ground for the church. In a similar vein, Rev. J. C. Taylor of the CMS noted in his Diary that just one week after his arrival at Onitsha, Nigeria twelve pupils were brought to him by their parents and guardians to be educated. To this, Taylor added: "I look upon them as the commencement of our missionary work. We lost no time but began to teach them the A.B.C." (Nduka, 1976, p. 70). Similarly, Rev. Hope Waddell established the Duke Town primary school in Calabar, Nigeria shortly after his arrival there in 1846. Rev. Samuel Crowther of the CMS opened a school at Onitsha immediately after he arrived in 1857. Indeed, Ajayi (1965) maintains that:

> The school was Crowther's chief method of evangelization. He introduced the mission into new places by getting rulers and elders interested in the idea of having a school of their own, and usually it was to the school that he asked the senior missionary at each station to give his chief attention. (p. 218)

T. J. Bowen of the Southern Baptist Convention believed that Christianity could not thrive without civilization. Hence, he proposed a three-tier system of education for Africa, namely literary, religious and technical (Afigbo, 1968, p. 199). And Father Shanahan commented:

> If we go from town to town talking only about God, we know from experience that much of our effort brings no result. But no one is opposed to school.(Father Shanahan cited in Ekechi, 1972, p. 176)

Missionaries turned their attention to the youths and schools as sources of conversion because they had come to realize to their utter dismay and dumbfoundment the futility of trying to convert men of good standing in Nigerian society because as Ekechi (1972) maintains, Nigerians complained that missionaries were interfering unduly with indigenous customs and practices. He goes on to add that, "to the majority of the indigenous population the revolutionary ideas propagated by the missionaries, . . . was justification enough to raise and alarm" (p. 173). However, the missionaries were more successful with the youths through the schools.

In a letter to Cardinal Golti in 1912, Bishop Shanahan wrote:

> The school keeps the missionary in contact with the people, because the children give him free entry into every house. He is no longer a stranger, but a member of the family. This fact alone makes what he can effect, and what he can prevent, really incalculable. He is known everywhere, and he alone (among Europeans) can go through the

country without danger. (Abernethy, 1969, p. 40)

Hence, in the words of Ekechi (1972), "formal education became the bait with which the young generation was enticed to Christianity" (p. 176). Good education, it was believed, would enable young men to earn a good living as well as enable them to exert their own influence and that of their denomination on the society at large. The chief proponents of evangelization through the schools, no doubt, were the Holy Ghost Fathers of the Roman Catholic Mission. Father Leon Lejeune, the Catholic Superior and the greatest advocate of this policy, once wrote to Msgr. LeRoy, in 1904 saying: "education is the only way ahead in Africa, there is no other possible way to convert the people" (Clarke, 1980, p. 51). Earlier, in 1901 he had said: "it is perilous to hesitate, the Christian village must go and all our concentration must be on the schools otherwise our enemy the Protestants will snatch the young" (Clarke, 1980, p. 51). In February 1903, Father Leon Lejeune again wrote: "Education is our principal work, and our hopes for the future are based on it" (Clarke, 1980, p. 52). In 1905, Father Shanahan, Lejeune's successor, wrote that, "it is through the schools that we will win over the whole country" (Clarke, 1980, p. 51). Indeed, in the same letter, he boasted that "he would use the Catholic schools to strike the last blow at the Presbyterians and others" (Clarke, 1980, p. 51).

The intense rivalry between the missions produced what one Holy Ghost Father called an "atmosphere of war" (Clarke, 1980, pp. 51-52), and the 1890s ushered in a school revolution in Southern Nigeria, for the fallout from the intense missionary rivalry was the establishment of an unprecedented number of mission schools. For example, the Church Missionary Society which started out with six schools in 1849 increased its number of schools to 150 by 1909 as follows (Table 3):

Table 3

Number of Church Missionary Society Schools and Scholars in Certain Years

Year	Number of Schools	Number of Scholars
1849	6	418
1859	6	553
1879	26	1,853
1889	52	2,672
1899	71	4,152
1909	150	9,561
1916	?	33,229

Source: P. Amaury Talbot, The Peoples of Southern Nigeria (London, 1969), IV, p. 128.

The Wesleyan Mission went from 3 schools, 255 pupils and 9 teachers in 1861 to 128 schools, 5,361 pupils and 285 teachers in 1921 (Table 4).

Table 4

Number of Wesleyan Schools and Teachers in Various Years

Year	Number of Schools	Scholars	Teachers & Evangelists
1861	3	255	9
1871	7	370	12
1881	16	631	33
1891	23	1,292	47
1901	26	1,188	49
1911	52	2,656	124
1921	128	5,361	285

Source: P. Amaury Talbot, The Peoples of Southern Nigeria (London, 1969), IV, p. 129.

And west of the Niger, the Roman Catholic Mission increased its number of schools from 2 in 1893 to about 127 in 1922. (See Table 5).

Table 5

Number of Roman Catholic Schools West of the Niger in Certain Years

Prefecture

Year	Bight of Benin No. of Schools	Western Nigeria No. of Schools	Niger No. of Schools
1893	-	2	?
1902	17	4	?
1912	42	14	?
1920	?	57	?
1922	70 (with 5,130 Scholars)	?	?

Source: P. Amaury Talbot, *The Peoples of Southern Nigeria* (London, 1969), IV, p. 130.

Abernethy (1969) makes the point that:

> The activity of the most education-minded denominations usually spurred the others to follow suit. For this reason school enrollment grew at a faster rate in Southern Nigeria with several missions operating than it might have with only one... (p. 44)

Explaining his contention further he wrote:

> For example, J. K. Coker, a leader in the breakaway African Church Movement, wrote in 1913: The plan of the Anglican Church of sending so many young men to college to qualify in Arts will surely place us at a disadvantage if these young men cannot be connected to the African Church or if the African Church does not pay great attention to education. (Abernethy, 1969, p. 44ff).

In Igboland as in other parts of Southern Nigeria, the school revolution played into the hands of anxious natives who had rightly come to associate Western education with the white man's physical power which was responsible for the destruction of his sovereignty and material world. Ayandele (1979) describes the collapse of "pagandom" in Igboland as follows:

> ...he (the Igboman) anxiously sought the aid of the missionary whom he looked to for enactment of expected miracles--the establishment

of the school and transformation of his children away from the indigenous world into 'book' people, the emerging new elite leaders who in the colonial setting were to share authority in Church and State. In the circumstances the missionary did not have to importune to be allowed to establish his enterprise. In the villages rather he was importuned by rival villages and communities for schools which came to be seen as the Open Sesame to the new world the Igbo were being led to envision... (p. 168)

Ayandele adds that:

So overwhelming was the enthusiasm of the Igbo for Christianity that the Church Missionary Society and the Society of the Holy Ghost Fathers, the two most important Christian missions to date in Igboland, found their human and material resources grossly inadequate for the unprecedented challenge. Hence the unending Macedonian call upon call on Salisbury Square and Propaganda Fide respectively. (Ayandele, 1979, p. 168)

Apart from Igboland, the education propaganda of the missions fell into the willing ears of Southern Nigerians who had, with good reasons, come to associate European technological achievement with Western education and were willing to pay the price for their desire to learn the secrets of white power. The excitement was so great that, writing in 1923, Talbot maintained:

An extraordinary longing for book-learning, and the power to speak and write English has invaded the native mind in the last few years; this appears to arise partly from a genuine wish for European culture and partly from a desire to raise themselves in the social scale and get away from manual work...(Talbot, 1969, p. 124)

Notice that during the ill-fated Niger expedition of 1841, for instance, Simon Jonas, a liberated slave of Igbo parentage, acted as an interpreter. At Abo the King Obi Ossai was so impressed when he saw Simon Jonas reading and interpreting the words of the Bible into Igbo language. He approached him, held him by his two hands and declared, "You must stay with me, you must teach me and my people the white man's letters: The white people can go up the river without you; they may leave you here until they return, or until others come" (Journal, 1842, p. 60). Recalling the incident much later, Rev. J. F. Schon noted in his journal of the Expedition up the Niger:

> I opened the English Bible, and made Simon Jonas read a few verses to him, and translate them in Ibo. The verses he read were some of the Beatitudes of our Saviour, in the fifth chapter of St. Matthew. Obi was uncommonly taken with this--that a White man could read and write was a matter of course, but that a Black man--an Ibo man--a slave in times past--should know this wonderful thing too, was more than he could ever have anticipated. (Journal, 1842, p. 60)

When they reached the junction of the Niger and Benue, they sent Simon Jonas back to the Obi where he stayed for three weeks as his guest. During this period Jonas taught the Bible, some English and needlework and also made clothes for the Obi. Indeed, at the end of the third week, there were about two hundred children in his "school". Before the party left Abo, the Obi requested for and was promised more teachers to come and teach him and his people (Ekechi, 1972, p. 3).

At Onitsha, the Igbos were fascinated with missionaries, not so much for trade or politics as Ekechi (1972) contends, but for learning, as Crowther observed thus:

> From all I could gather by observation, the Ibos are very emulative: as in other things, so it will be in book-learning. Other towns will not rest satisfied until they have also learned the mystery of reading and writing, by which their neighbors may surpass or put them in the shade. (Ekechi, 1972, p. 7)

Not surprisingly therefore, as early as 1896 a CMS Superintendent, P. A. Bennett, reported from Obosi in Nigeria as follows:

> People are burning with the desire to learn; they give us little or no rest. We are obliged to be keeping school three times a day; the big men show interest and are trying to learn with all their might...Our house is generally crowded to suffocation. (Ekechi, 1972, p. 178; Ayandele 1979, p. 169)

Little wonder, therefore, that in 1905 the CMS mission Secretary wrote to complain about the pathetic nature of his work arising from the competition of Igbo villages for schools and learning. He stated his case as follows:

> My work is pathetic in the extreme now, in one aspect: almost every week I have to turn away deputations from towns both near and distant begging us to come and teach them. (Ayandele, 1979, p. 169)

The Roman Catholic Mission and the School Revolution in Nigeria

Missionary rivalry in Nigeria took a whole new meaning when the Roman Catholic mission entered the missionary field in Eastern Nigeria. The Holy Ghost Fathers who were put in charge of the Lower Niger started work first at Onitsha in 1885 with the arrival of Father Lutz as Superior of Holy Trinity mission at Onitsha. In that same year, Father Lutz opened a mission at Onitsha on a piece of land donated by the Obi of Onitsha through the instrumentality of Bishop Crowther. Under Father Joseph Shanahan (later Bishop), the Catholic mission spread its variety of religion and education to most parts of Igbo, Ibibio and Ogoja provinces east of the Niger. In order to do this, Shanahan drew up two phases of evangelization programs. The first phase was the "Christian village phase", which consisted of attempts to create Christian villages made up of converts. The next phase was the "village school phase", by which Father Shanahan took the school to the villages. In his belief that the school could serve as the best instrument for the evangelization of the society, Father Shanahan built schools in nearly every village under his jurisdiction. The village school became an avowed policy of the Holy Ghost Fathers. Indeed, as early as the 1900s when Father Leon Lejeune took over from Father Lutz as the Catholic Superior, the policy of evangelization through the school had become the mission's tactical approach to evangelization, for Father Lejeune saw education both as a means of spreading Christianity and as a means of ensuring Catholic dominance. Consequently, he made great efforts to increase student intake in Catholic schools throughout Eastern Nigeria. He believed that good education would enable the students to earn a good living as well as exert their influence in society to the Roman Catholic favor. When Father Shanahan took over from Father Lejeune, he expressed a similar concern. Hence, he wrote:

> I realized suddenly that when the children had been baptized in the schools they would go back to their pagan homes...Who would doubt that through these tiny apostles, mothers and fathers would come to know God. (Ekechi, 1972, p. 177)

However, the "village school" succeeded where the "Christian villages" failed. Consequently, there was an upsurge of Catholic schools particularly in Igboland. Statistics show that in 1906, there were 26 Catholic schools; in 1912, thirty-six, but in 1919, 310 of them (Solaru, 1964, p. 15). This policy resulted in the expansion of the Catholic faith in Eastern Nigeria as the schools served as avenues for the evangelization of the local population. To ensure the success of the village schools, a Teacher Training College[12] was opened in Igbariam in 1913. Though the school was closed down in 1918 as a result of the First World War, it was reopened in 1928 at Onitsha as St. Charles' Training College. In its evangelization program, teachers, catechists and pupils were all involved. In some instances, teachers were trained by attaching pupils to missionaries as apprentices. Between 1909 and 1910, twenty such teachers were trained and in 1912 fifty of them were produced. In every case, each teacher was assigned sixty pupils. By 1919, however, the number of Catholic schools in Southern Nigeria had increased to 310 including two assisted secondary schools, St. Gregory's College, Lagos and Christ the King's College, Onitsha (Solaru, 1964, p. 15).

For the Catholics, education was the best means by which Roman Catholic influence and prestige could be firmly established in Nigeria. Indeed, for some of them the school was the only hope for the realization of their missionary aspirations and objectives. Father Lena, the Superior at Calabar in Nigeria summed up the views of those who regarded education as a handmaid of proselytization in his memorandum of 1910 as follows:

> I think anybody who condemns the school as a way to gain the people to our religion is to be blamed. The results are there which are very consoling and encouraging. It is the way which has been chosen in our mission, it is good, it ought to be kept not half and half, but on a footing the best as possible... Theoretically people can be evangelized

without schools and as I read once, Our Savior did not send the Apostles to teach but to preach. But practically it is impossible to get on without schools... Let us keep our schools which God is blessing so far... (Ekechi, 1972, pp. 193-194).

At a time when there were pressing demands for secondary schools among the Protestant missions, Father Shanahan was very disturbed about a possible loss of Catholic leadership in education. He was also disturbed about the consequences of students from Government and Protestant schools gaining political leadership in the country. He lamented about the future of Catholics if graduates from Protestant and Government schools were to rule the country as political leaders. He pondered aloud over the fate of Roman Catholics if more opportunities for higher education existed only in Protestant and Government schools (Ekechi, 1972, p. 194). To him, should this happen, then the Catholic influence would be significantly reduced (Ekechi, 1971, p. 194). In order to have Catholics represented in the political arena of the country, Father Shanahan appealed to his congregation in 1909 to provide the resources necessary to enable him to establish an advanced school for the training of political leaders (Ekechi, 1972, p. 194). "If this is not done," he lamented, "the victory will go to the adversaries" (Ekechi, 1972, p. 194). In 1910, he prepared a memorandum on higher education in which he maintained quite forcefully that the Bonny Government College had all Protestant teachers on its staff, which in effect means that Roman Catholic children who go there would turn Protestants. This was inconceivable to the Catholics' most powerful man in Eastern Nigeria. "We are not going to send our children there," he noted, "never would we ever send any of our children there" (Ekechi, 1972, p. 194). As for the Hope Waddell Training Institution, Father Shanahan noted that it was already a Protestant institution to which no Catholic child should go. Stating his case for financial support to establish an advanced college for Catholic children, he maintained that as for evangelization and social change, the college would repay a hundredfold all that was spent on it, and from the intellectual standpoint, the college would certainly be a center of learning--a quasi university for Southern Nigeria (Ekechi, 1972, p. 195).

Father Shanahan's appeal was not without its effect, for within a short time, money and resources were made available for the establishment of an advanced Roman Catholic school at Onitsha where Greek, Latin, Mathematics and other academic subjects were taught. (This school appears to have been an equivalent of the lower and upper sixth forms).

The Founding of Dennis Memorial Grammar School (D M G S), Onitsha

The founding of Dennis Memorial Grammar School is of special interest here because it is a classical example of the outcome of missionary rivalry in Nigeria. During the period under study, there were noticeable differences between the Church Missionary Society (CMS) run schools and those of the Roman Catholic Mission (RCM). Of outstanding significance was the fact that the Roman Catholics taught the English language in their schools from the early grades while the CMS frowned upon the teaching of the English language in their own schools. The teaching of English was of particular attraction to students and parents alike because in the colonial situation competency in the English language was necessary as a means of reaping "the material advantages of English Education" (Ekechi, 1972, p. 178). The refusal by the CMS to include the teaching of the English language in their curriculum derived from an earlier memorandum drafted in 1890 which stated that:

> The teaching in the mission schools should be of the simplest kind-- the chief aim of which being to teach the children to read in the vernacular, so that they may be able to study their Bibles when translated for them in the mother tongue. (Ekechi, 1972, p. 180)

Perceiving the threat posed by the Roman Catholic curriculum to the CMS missionary field, particularly the teaching of the English language, Archdeacon Dennis, the CMS Mission Secretary in Nigeria, in a letter to Baylis, the CMS London Secretary, in 1899, pleaded passionately for the inclusion of the English language in the CMS school curriculum and for the establishment of a CMS secondary school at

Onitsha. "It will be a very great pity," he maintained, "if they (Roman Catholics) are first in the field..." (Ekechi, 1972, p. 181). When it came to his notice that some parents were anxious to send their children to Roman Catholic schools where the English language was taught, Dennis wrote to his mission headquarters in London about the proverbial wisdom of lifting the ban on the teaching of the English language in CMS schools and on modifying the CMS stand on secular education because "if they (the Protestants) cannot get what they want with us (sic) they will go to the Romanists" (Ekechi, 1972, p. 182). In every case, however, Dennis' advice fell on deaf ears.

A more serious dimension was added to the problem of the CMS when the Roman Catholics established a High School at Onitsha in 1901. The Catholic High School was particularly attractive to parents and students because, apart from industrial education, the curriculum included elementary Algebra, Geometry, Book Keeping and Foreign Languages. The establishment of the Catholic High School according to Ekechi (1972) "stirred the CMS missionaries to action" (p. 185). From now on, there were persistent pressure from CMS missionaries in the field to their mission headquarters in London for action. In a letter to Baylis in 1901, Alvarez, the local Secretary at Onitsha, Nigeria, said:

> Now that the Roman Catholics had already started a high school in the town, it was about time steps were taken to open a CMS secondary school to forestall a Roman Catholic bid for the control of education. (Ekechi, 1972, p. 185)

Indeed, in 1911, a local Secretary of the CMS had this to tell his London office:

> To cope with the growing demand for education we shall need at Onitsha a boys' boarding school--or secondary school; otherwise we shall find that the Roman Catholics will attract many of our boys by the offer of a more advanced education than we can give in our ordinary school. (Ekechi, 1972, p. 196)

As a matter of fact, calls from the CMS missionaries were persistent and unequivocal because the scare created by the establishment of the Roman Catholic High School had reached a fever pitch. So much was it that Bishop Tugwell, the CMS Bishop of Western Equatorial Africa, whose jurisdiction included the Niger Mission, wrote to G. T. Basden, the then Acting Secretary of the Niger Mission, to complain that young people in search of education were moving to Onitsha in large numbers from the hinterland. He lamented that:

> The Romanists realized this, and...are directing all their energies to the interest of education, striving by all means to direct the stream into their own channels, and apparently with marked success...There is no denying the fact that at the present moment nearly all the young people of Onitsha Town and Waterside who attend school are to be found in the Roman Schools. (Nduka, 1976, p. 79)

With figures from government reports and mission inspectors, Bishop Tugwell was able to support his contention. As a counter measure to Roman Catholic popularity and dominance, a situation he considered "fraught with grave danger to the Native Church of the Future" (Nduka, 1976, p. 79), he suggested that the Awka Training College should be removed to Onitsha and that a CMS High School should be opened adjacent to the Training College. Although the suggestion for the removal of the Awka Training College was rejected, given the tempo and feelings of the moment, the Executive Committee of the Niger Mission, in its meeting of January 30 to February 7, 1911, deviated from its age-old policy of a "return to indigenous life-style", and accepted in principle the establishment of "a thoroughly equipped Central School at Onitsha with Elementary and Secondary Departments" (Nduka, 1976, p. 80). While the Executive Committee of the Niger Mission approved the opening of the High School in principle, the physical foundation of the school eluded the mission until 1925 due to financial and other reasons. Nduka (1976) maintains:

> The opening of Dennis Memorial Grammar School (D.M.G.S.) (was) not unconnected with the vicissitudes of the rivalry... The origins of D.M.G.S. are traceable, at least in part, to the attempt of the C.M.S. authorities of the Niger Mission to escape from the dilemma into which their previous policies had landed them. They thought that the establishment of a grammar school would give them an upper hand over their archrivals--the Roman Catholic Holy Ghost Fathers. (Pp. 69 & 73)

Missionary Rivalry West of the Niger

It is necessary to emphasize here that it is untrue to say that there were no interdenominational rivalries in Yorubaland. When Methodist residents of Lagos wanted the Wesleyan Methodist Society to open a secondary school for their children, this is how they put their case in 1874:

> The majority of the community of this town have directly or indirectly been brought under the influence of the teaching of Methodism, but on account of the facilities which are generally afforded by the Church Missionary Society as regards the higher standard of education, many of our people, who have passed under its teaching, have become Churchmen...(because of) the necessity of their being sent to the Church Missionary Society Grammar School... The result is, after their training, it always becomes very difficult with them to shake off the prejudice which they have imperceptibly imbibed against that Church with which their parents had the honour and privilege to be connected. (Abernethy, 1969, p. 44)

What is true then is that interdenominational rivalry west of the Niger was much more subtle because Yoruba towns like Lagos, Abeokuta, Ibadan, Ijebu-Ode and Oyo were far too large for a single denomination to be able to meet all its needs-- religious and educational. And in smaller towns, different denominations acquired rights of occupancy to specific areas; the Baptists were at Ogbomosho, the Methodist at Ijebu-Remo, the CMS at Ondo and Ekiti. In the west of Nigeria, Protestants came first and in every case Catholics were late comers. Be it at Ijebu territory, in Ado-Ekiti or Ondo, Protestants' numerical superiority gave them a clear advantage over their Catholic rivals. Besides, Catholic priests sent to Western Nigeria belonged to the Société des Missions Africaines who spoke French instead of English and most of whose members believed in direct apostolate instead of the use of schools as a means of evangelization. Also, in the west, apart from the existence of many denominations, there was the Muslim Advance from the north as well as the real visible presence of the independent African Churches. The struggle for missionary fields, therefore, had many dimensions and was not as sharp as the struggle between Protestants and Catholics in Eastern Nigeria. However, missionary rivalry existed west of the Niger as it did in the east.

It is important to make the point that in the educational game, the Yorubas of the west far outplayed the Igbos of the east between 1921 and 1931 as Table 6 shows, but this advantage did not last for a long time as the Igbos soon caught up with the Yorubas.

Table 6

Enrollment as a Percentage of School-Age Population by Province, 1921 and 1931

Province	1921	1931
Western Region:		
Lagos and Colony	28.4%	39.5%
Abeokuta	6.3	7.4
Benin	4.0	10.3
Ijebu	16.7	13.0
Ondo	4.8	7.3
Oyo	2.3	4.4
Warri	6.2	10.4
Eastern Region:		
Calabar	20.4	30.2
Ogoja	2.3	1.5
Onitsha	9.3	11.8
Owerri	5.5	13.5
British Cameroons	1.8	10.4
All Provinces	9.2	12.5

Source: David B. Abernethy (1969) "The Political Dilemma of Popular Education" (Stanford CA, Stanford University Press). p. 37.

The reason for the earlier disparity in education between the east and west is that the area west of the Niger was blessed with indigenous educated elites most of whom had graduated from Training Institutions in Lagos and from Fourah Bay College after 1876. These were the men who spread education and Christianity in Ijebuland for instance. They were people like Charles Phillipses, Rev. Ransome

Kuti, Ogumefun and Gonsallos. There were others who were redeemed during the Yoruba wars, who were educated at Ibadan and Abeokuta; who took education and Christianity to Eastern Yoruba country. Notable among them were the Babamubonis, the Atundaolus and the Laseindes (Ayandele, 1979, p. 174). Thus, unlike in Igboland, the Yoruba country had an educated corps of its own. These Western-educated Sierra Leone immigrants were instrumental to the founding of some secondary schools. The CMS Grammar School, Lagos founded in 1859 and the Methodist Boys' High School founded in 1878 by Yoruba clergymen, are illustrative of this point. Thus, out of twenty-six secondary schools and teacher training institutions established in Southern Nigeria before 1930, three were established at the Onitsha and Asaba axis, two in Calabar and seven at Lagos. By the first two decades of this century, however, the Igbos had begun to catch up with the Yorubas and by the 1960s were at parity with them. Here is what Ayandele (1979) has to say on this:

> By 1960 the social and cultural miracle which the Igbo expected from Christianity had been definitely achieved. They could console themselves with the belief that in their game of educational catch-up they had achieved quantitative parity with the Yoruba, their chief rival, who had two generations of opportunity before the Igbo. Although demographically two million less than the Yoruba, they boast of as many primary and secondary grammar schools, as many undergraduates, as many pen-pushers and technocrats, as many professionals in law, engineering, and the world of business. By 1960 the Igbo had contributed many leaders to the Nigerian political scene, including the most popular national political figure, Nnamdi Azikiwe... (p. 178)

By 1921, however, there were 2,243 schools, 137,235 pupils and 3,683 teachers in mission-operated schools in Southern Nigeria distributed as shown in Table 7.

As Table 8 shows, there were twenty-six Secondary and Teacher Training Institutions founded in Southern Nigeria between 1859 and 1930.

Table 7
Number of Schools, Students, and Teachers in Southern Nigeria, by Province and Township, 1921

Province	Government Schools	Scholars	Teachers	Assisted Schools	Scholars	Teachers	Non-Asst Schools	Scholars	Teachers	Total Schools	Scholars	Teachers
Lagos Colony	4	830	23	26	4,532	163	67	7,439	190	97	12,811	376
Abeokuta	-	-	-	15	2,093	76	56	2,166	61	71	4,259	137
Benin	14	1,766	50	6	533	35	54	3,498	93	74	5,797	187
Calabar	8	759	27	19	4,190	224	643	35,655	725	670	40,604	976
Ijebu	-	-	-	18	3,084	106	89	3,683	121	107	6,767	227
Ogoja	1	33	2	11	847	49	27	1,587	32	39	2,467	83
Ondo	1	309	13	13	633	31	76	2,663	97	90	3,605	131
Onitsha	3	643	18	6	746	46	367	26,599	599	376	27,988	663
Owerri	8	770	35	8	1,001	51	473	20,328	607	489	22,099	693
Oyo	1	110	6	15	1,135	59	117	3,879	152	133	5,124	217
Warri	3	735	21	2	402	17	80	3,490	112	85	4,627	150
Cameroons	8	927	18	-	-	-	4	170	5	12	1,097	23
All Provinces	51	6,882	212	139	19,196	857	2,053	111,157	2,794	2,243	137,235	3,863

Source: P. Amaury Talbot, "The Peoples of Southern Nigeria" (London, 1969) IV, p. 131

Table 8

**Secondary and Teacher Training Institutions
Founded in Southern Nigeria, 1859-1930**

School	Location	Date	Agency
C.M.S. Grammar School	Lagos	1859	C.M.S.
St. Gregory's College	Lagos	1876	R.C.M.
Methodist Boys' High School	Lagos	1878	Methodist
Methodist Girls' High School	Lagos	1879	Methodist
Baptist Boys' High School	Lagos	1885	Baptist
Hope Waddell Training Institute	Calabar, E.R.	1895	C.S.M.
St. Andrew's College	Oyo, W.R.	1896	C.M.S.
Baptist Training College	Ogbomosho, W.R.	1897	Baptist
St. Paul's Training College	Awka, E.R.	1904	C.M.S.
Oron Training Institute	Oron, E.R.	1905	Prim. Meth.
Wesleyan Training Institute	Ibadan, W.R.	1905	Methodist
Abeokuta Grammar School	Abeokuta, W.R.	1908	C.M.S.
King's College	Lagos	1909	Government
Eko Boys' High School	Lagos	1913	Private
Ibadan Grammar School	Ibadan, W.R.	1913	C.M.S.
Ijebu-Ode Grammar School	Ijebu-Ode, W.R.	1913	C.M.S.
Duke Town Secondary School	Calabar, E.R.	1919	C.S.M.
Ondo Boys' High School	Ondo, W.R.	1919	C.M.S.
Ibo Boys' Institute	Uzuakoli, E.R.	1923	Prim. Meth.
Baptist Boys' High School	Abeokuta, W.R.	1923	Baptist
Dennis Memorial Grammar School	Onitsha, E.R.	1928	C.M.S.
United Missionary College	Ibadan, W.R.	1928	C.M.S.-Meth.
St. Thomas' College	Asaba, W.R.	1928	R.C.M.
St. Charles' Training College	Onitsha, E.R.	1929	R.C.M.
Government College	Umuahia, E.R.	1929	Government
Government College	Ibadan, W.R.	1929	Government

*Source: David B. Abernethy, The Political Dilemma of Popular Education,
(Stanford, CA 1969) p. 36.*

The Results of Church and Christian Missionary Rivalry in Nigeria

As we have seen, the intense rivalry between the missions produced what one Holy Ghost Father called an "atmosphere of war" (Clarke, 1980, pp. 51-52), and as Nduka (1979) contends:

> The opening of Dennis Memorial Grammar School...(was) not unconnected with the vicissitudes of the rivalry ... The origins of D.M.G.S. are traceable, at least in part, to the attempt of the C.M.S. authorities of the Niger Mission to escape from the dilemma into which their previous policies had landed them. They thought that the establishment of a grammar school would give them an upper hand over their arch rivals-the Roman Catholic Holy Ghost Fathers. (pp. 69, 73)

The fallout from the intense missionary rivalry in Southern Nigeria ushered forth a school revolution, and an unprecedented number of mission schools were established there during the late 19th and early 20th centuries. As Abernethy (1969) attests:

> The activity of the most education-minded denominations usually spurred the others to follow suit. For this reason school enrollment grew at a faster rate in southern Nigeria with several missions operating than it might have with only one... (p. 44)

The CMS started out with 6 schools in 1849 and increased that number to 150 by 1909 (see Table 3). The RCM increased its number of schools from 2 in 1893 to about 127 in 1922 (see Table 5). Other denominations also established schools. As Table 4 shows, the Wesleyan Mission went from 3 schools, 255 pupils, and 9 teachers in 1861 to 138 schools, 5,361 pupils, and 285 teachers by 1921. Hence, by 1921, there were 2,192 schools, 130,353 pupils, and 3,651 teachers in mission-operated schools in Southern Nigeria (see Table 7). Additionally, 26 secondary and teacher training institutions were founded in the region between 1859 and 1930 (Table 8).

The educational propaganda of the missions fell upon the receptive ears of the people of Southern Nigeria, who came to associate European technological achievement with Western education and who were willing to pay the price to learn the secrets of White power. Apart from being the source of this power, formal education conferred several definite advantages to the colonized Nigerians. The consolidation of British control, for instance, created opportunities for European-trained Nigerians because literate indigenous men were needed to fill minor administrative positions. Moreover, the churches needed teachers and catechists, and business concerns needed clerks, accountants, buyers, and sales representatives. Consequently, a European education soon came to be viewed by Southern Nigerians themselves as an investment and an exciting opportunity. Writing in 1923, Talbot maintained the following:

> An extraordinary longing for book-learning, and the power to speak and write English has invaded the native mind in the last few years; this appears to arise partly from a genuine wish for European culture and partly from a desire to raise themselves in the social scale and get away from manual work. (Talbot, 1969, p. 124)

It is important to note that during the period covered in this study the rate of expansion of Western education in Southern Nigeria contrasted drastically with that of Northern Nigeria. By 1921 there were only 103 Christian-run primary schools, with 2,964 pupils and 162 teachers, in Northern Nigeria despite its larger land mass (Meek, 1969, p. 263). In 1937 Northern Nigeria had 549 primary schools with a total enrollment of 20,269 pupils and only one secondary school serving 65 students (see Bray, 1981, p. 17). In Northern Nigeria, however, church and missionary rivalries were almost nonexistent due to the British colonial government's official policy of restricting Christian missionaries to non-Muslim areas discussed earlier in this book. For this and other reasons stated below, the development of Western education was painfully slow in the Nigerian North, while intense missionary and church rivalry in the South led to its rapid expansion.

Why Christian Missionary Education Was a Dismal Failure in Northern Nigeria

I have already discussed the British colonial government's official policy of restricting Christian missionaries to non-Muslim areas of the north, for in a country where the school was an adjunct of the church, such a policy had disastrous consequences for Western education in the north. Another reason why Christian missionary education failed woefully in Northern Nigeria is that Islam and Islamic education which were introduced into Northern Nigeria in the fifteenth century had been heavily entrenched before the coming of the Europeans (Fafunwa, 1974, Clarke, 1978, p. 134). By 1919, a well orchestrated system of Islamic education was already in place in Northern Nigeria with an estimated 25,000 Islamic scholars and about 250,000 students (Fafunwa, 1974, Clarke, 1978). A literary class known as mallamai had emerged. This group formed the administrative corps of native authority administration throughout Northern Nigeria. The colonial government report on Northern Nigeria of 1919 recorded that the mallamai were a "very influential class, some of them very well read in Arabic literature and law and deeply imbued with the love of learning" (Clarke, 1978, p. 134).

By 1945, there were about 30,000 Islamic scholars with about 20,000 Islamic schools in Northern Nigeria (Fafunwa, 1974; Clarke, 1978). In addition, there were about 2,777 Islamic secondary schools (ilm) with about 36,000 students throughout Northern Nigeria where Islamic law, Arabic grammar, mysticism, moral ethos, ethics, customs and traditions of Islamic society were studied. Through the years, there had developed in Northern Nigeria an educational system which was not only acceptable but which was considered by most northerners as superior to Western education (Ayandele, 1967, 1980). According to Doi (1978, p. 334), "Islam provided believers with a Universalist religion, an Islamic social and religious pattern, and an attitude of cultural and religious superiority over Pagans (and Christians)." The introduction of Western education into Northern Nigeria was vehemently challenged because Western education was considered not only as counter-culture and counter-Islam, but missionaries were perceived as pathfinders of European imperialism. Secondly, Muslims were unwilling to forego a well organized system of Islamic education for an ill-organized and an uncertain one. Also, Western education, it was feared, would affect the whole social, religious, political, cultural, ethical and psychological fabric of Northern Nigerian society. Besides, the roles and means of livelihood of the mallamai (Muslim teachers) were threatened. Muslims, therefore, did not want to adopt a system of education for which they had great contempt. Indeed, from 1906, even the British administration in Northern Nigeria was anti-missionary. (It is instructive to point out that Christian missionaries were the forebearers of Western education in Nigeria before 1970. Resentment of missionaries meant resentment of Western education as well). According to Ayandele (1980, p. 147), "Education along Western lines was frowned upon as a disintegrating and demoralizing agency..." Indeed, a Kano poet wrote to say that Christian schools "are not beneficial at all and there is nothing in them but lies, evil and paganism... They have also established churches so that they might lead the people astray" (cited in Clarke, 1978, p. 134). Consequently, the Emirs did not allow missionaries to build schools in their territories (Fafunwa, 1974; Ayandele, 1967, 1980; Clarke, 1978). Indeed, anti-missionary sentiments reached fever pitch in Northern Nigeria during the period covered by this book and fear of a Mahdist uprising gripped most British officials. In the words of one Kano trader, the coming of the British and Christian missionaries was a sign of the "last days" (Clarke, 1978, 134). As another Kano Muslim trader wrote:

> There is evidence indicating imminent appearance of the Mahdi. Among the proofs are the coming of the Europeans to Hausaland...Emirs have no power but they go to Kaduna...legal cases will not be dealt with by the Qu'ran...sons of Ulama go about like Pagans from one end of the country to the other without any guidance...they cut their hair like Christians. Many women go about with their heads uncovered...a boy will not be obedient to his parents and one who is learned will not tell the truth. The Christians prevent all things.(Clarke, 1978, p. 134)

It is important also to note that the Northern Emirs were uncompromising adherents of the tenets of Islam (Ayandele, 1967, 1980). Indeed, as the political and religious leaders of their people, the Emirs were required by Muslim law to protect the religion, for not to do so would be apostasy -- a great sin. Fafunwa (1974) captures this point well when he states that, "all the northern Emirs were political and spiritual leaders of their people and would not tolerate any local or foreign interference" (p. 100). He went on to add that, "the advent of Christianity in Nigeria in 1842 caused a head-on collision with Islam, especially in the north where it was more firmly established." It is indeed difficult to dispute the religious obligations of the Emirs because in their letters of appointment as Emirs by the Shaikh Uthman dan Fodio, the Shaikh emphasized more than anything else their religious obligations. In his letter of appointment, Yaqub, the Emir of Bauchi was enjoined:

> (i) to be consistent and stand by what he says and commands; (ii) to be zealous in maintaining mosques; (iii) to be zealous in praying there; (iv) to study the Quran and its teachings; (v) to study the (Islamic) sciences and their teachings; (vi) to maintain the markets and prevent illegalities there; (vii) to wage the jihad. (Last, 1967, p.56)

Britain's Laissez-Faire Educational Policy and Its Consequences for the Nigerian Educational System

The most striking feature of colonial educational policy in Nigeria before 1882 was Britain's reluctance to bear its cost and her limited and indirect role in it. Indeed, during the period in question, government participation in education was limited to a meagre £600 shared between the three missionary bodies engaged in some form of educational enterprise in Nigeria. But, since the missions saw education as an effective means of conversion each began its educational work as soon as its initial grounds were cleared. This evangelistic objective for education was not without its cost or repercussions for the Nigerian educational system. In the first place, since there was no government control of schools before 1901, not one of the missions had any coordination of its scattered schools. It was not until 1901 that the first Inspector of Education was appointed for Southern Nigeria. On the state of the schools before 1901, Gordon, the first British Inspector of Education for Southern Nigeria, had this to say:

> Until recently there was little organization even among the schools maintained by one mission. In most cases the management of each

> appears to have been left entirely in the hands of the local representative of the mission. (Afigbo, 1968, p. 198)

And since there was no central control of schools by the government, the missions had no compelling reasons to submit periodic reports outlining the progress of their work. Also, as we have seen, the motive behind the early introduction of Western education by missions was the evangelistic one of spreading the gospel and as long as this objective was fulfilled, the aim of education for the missions was said to have been achieved.

What, we may ask, were the consequences for education of mission control of schools in Nigeria up to and including 1900? Afigbo (1968) answers this question very succinctly when he says:

> The virtual missionary monopoly of education in nineteenth century Southern Nigeria left its mark on the system of education which the Southern Nigeria Administration inherited from the Niger Coast Protectorate in 1900. All the schools remained modest establishments indeed and tended to share the same merits and demerits. (p. 200)

The earliest schools were modest ones indeed. In one sense, they were the type where a missionary kept a school at home with student teachers who were like apprentices forming part of his household. Schoolmasters were poorly educated thereby affecting the quality of education in the mission schools. As one Mission Secretary once put it, "the standard of education was so low that neither the teachers themselves nor the students could pass Government examinations which required some degree of knowledge in depth" (Ekechi, 1972, p. 188). Indeed, even Mission reports confirm the deplorable state of teachers at this time. In one such report, it was stated:

> The prevalent anxiety for teaching leads to some dangers. When the Mission cannot supply teachers, the people are apt to engage lads of doubtful character... These lads undertake the work merely for the sake of what they can get; they have had no training and are under no supervision; and three have lately been imprisoned for aiding and abetting the people in opposition to the Government. Efforts are made to increase the efficiency of such young teachers by sending them to

> Kaiyama for training, but the plan unsettles the men, and they are inclined to look upon the time of their residence at Kaiyama as a sort of holiday. (Solaru, 1964, p. 23)

The curriculum of the Teacher Training Institutions consisted mainly of religious instruction since the "schools" were designed to train teacher-evangelists. It was not until the 1890s that some of the missions tried to make their schools more secular and also established some form of supervision. The CMS went first by appointing an inspector, aimed at centralized control of its schools and "adopted a modified form of the educational code of Barbados, West Indies..." (Afigbo, 1968, p. 201). In 1895, the Presbyterian mission in Calabar took definite steps to secularize education by establishing the Hope Waddell Training Institution where students "could be given higher education of a general character as well as special instruction in certain branches of industrial work" (Nwabara, 1977, p. 61). This was indeed the first real attempt at secular education because a board of education was established for Hope Waddell in which its principal sat along with other members to formulate policies for the school (Nwabara, 1977, p. 61).

Colonial Government Intervention in Education

Despite her reluctance to bear its cost, the British government considered education important enough to merit its attention. In 1901, for instance, Sir Ralph Moor, the British Consul-General in Nigeria, explained the British Government's position on education in Nigeria as follows:

> I would submit that the provision of adequate opportunities for the Natives is one of the primary duties revolving on local administrations consequent on the powers assumed by Her Majesty's Government in Nigeria and one that required and is deserving of immediate attention. As a matter of policy it is a duty that should be at once coped with for permanent peace cannot be established in the territories until enlightenment and education are introduced and the untutored savage is taught and disciplined in methods of earning a regular livelihood by supplying the wants and demands of his neighbours--Native and European--instead of relying on Nature and seizing his neighbours' goods for one. Further the administration and

> merchants are at present hampered by want of trained clerks, artisans, etc. and capital is drained from the territories in salaries paid to foreign natives who spend as little as possible therein. (Afigbo, 1968, p. 200)

Accordingly, government responded to the challenge of poor academic performance of mission schools by enacting the Education Ordinance of 1881 which covered the West African territories of Lagos, the Gold Coast, Sierra Leone and the Gambia. In 1887, another Education Ordinance was enacted in which schools not only received grants-in-aid but provisions were made for the granting of teacher's certificates. This Ordinance was followed by the 1903 Education Code for Southern Nigeria. The Education Code of 1903 had far reaching consequences for education because in it evolved a:

> system under which the primary schools could be relied upon for giving a systematic education in the lower standards to a sufficient number of scholars to render it possible to establish and maintain schools for the higher standards large enough to justify the engagement of a thoroughly competent teaching staff. (Nwabara, 1977, p. 61)

The Code provided for a three tier system of education--namely primary, intermediate and high school. The 1903 Education Code was followed by the 1916 Grants Code. To qualify for annual grants, a school was to meet specific requirements and grants were made on the following conditions.

- 30 per cent for tone, discipline, organization and moral instruction of the school
- 20 per cent for adequate and efficient staff
- 10 per cent for building, equipment and sanitation
- 40 per cent on the results of periodical examinations and general progress.

The 1916 Education Code replaced grants on "payment by results" with grants on "general efficiency of a school." From now on, the need for government to spend more money on education was the more recognized.

The Education Code of 1926 abrogated completely the practice of paying grants on the basis of examination results and replaced it with an assessment on the basis of efficiency. Schools were henceforth classified as grades A, B, C, or D, depending on the amount of salaries paid and the size of the school. The Code also:

1. Required that teachers must be registered as a condition for teaching in any school in Southern Nigeria (Colony and Southern Provinces).

2. Forbade the opening of a school unless approved by the Director of Education and the board of education.

3. Authorized the closing of a school if it was being conducted in a manner not in the interest of the people or the community where it was located.

4. Defined the functions and duties of supervisors or mission inspectors.

5. Expanded and strengthened the existing board of education by including the Director and the Deputy Director of Education, the Assistant Director, ten representatives of the mission and other educational agencies; and redefined the board's functions to include advice to the government on educational matters.

6. Regulated minimum pay for teachers employed in an assisted school. (Fafunwa, 1974, 126)

In addition, missions were allowed to appoint their own school supervisors and managers.

The Phillipson Grants-in-Aid of Education in Nigeria of 1948 and its revised version of 1955 were designed (a) to increase government participation in education, (b) to share cost in education between the public and private sectors, (c) to adjust zonal contributions by the private sector and (d) to define the commitments of voluntary agencies to education.

Nationalist Governments and the Introduction of the Universal Primary Education Schemes in the 1950s

Following the Macpherson Constitution of 1951 which created the Regional Houses of Assembly and empowered them to appropriate funds and make laws in specific areas such as health, education, agriculture and local governments, the West and East Regional governments embarked on Universal Primary Education programs in 1955 and 1957, respectively.

The Western Regional government[13] started its scheme on January 17, 1955. Within the first year of its implementation, primary school enrollment in Western Nigeria rose from 457,000 in 1954 to 811,000 in 1955, that is, from 31% to 61%. Also, the number of primary school teachers rose from 17,000 in 1954 to 27,000 in 1955 and the number of primary schools increased by 30% (Adamu, 1973, pp. 49-50). These were no mean achievements particularly when it is observed that the Western State budget on education jumped from £2.2 million in 1954 to £5.4 million in 1955.

The East Regional government started its own Universal Primary Education program in 1957. As in the West, the first year of the scheme witnessed a tremendous increase in enrollments from 775,000 pupils in 1956 to 1,209,000 in 1957. This represents an enrollment increase of 25%. The number of teachers in primary schools rose from 30,000 in 1956 to 41,000 in 1957, and the number of primary schools increased from 5,060 to 6,986. Education expenditure increased from £3.6 million in 1956 to £6 million in 1957 (Adamu, 1973, p. 50).

Although due to financial constraints, poor planning, administrative inexperience and corruption, parts of the plan were either scaled down or abandoned altogether, it nevertheless ushered in a period of education awareness in Southern Nigeria.

While the two Southern States were busy planning or executing their Universal Primary Education schemes, the Northern Region concentrated its efforts in the development of Adult education which was popularly called Campaign Against Ignorance. The Campaign Against Ignorance program was officially launched in 1952. Out of 79,000 adults who enrolled in the program in 1952-53, 19,000 were awarded certificates. The organizers of the program envisioned that if they could run 15,000 classes of two sessions annually, they would attain general adult literacy by

1957 or 1958 (Bray, 1981, p. 51). Like the Universal Primary Education schemes in the West and the East, adult education in the North ran into difficulties although some remarkable achievements were made in this area. For one thing, adult education received the priority which it had not previously received and was not to receive again until much later.

CHAPTER V

GOVERNMENT TAKE-OVER OF SCHOOLS IN NIGERIA

As was noted earlier, the 1951 Macpherson constitution empowered the Regions to appropriate funds for, among other things, education. In 1954 education in Nigeria was regionalized. Each region of the federation passed education laws and ordinances. The West and the East attempted Universal Primary education while the North concentrated its efforts on the development of adult education. As a guide to future policies on education, several commissions were set up at the regional and federal levels. Whether it was Ashby, Dike, Ikoku, Asabia, Adefarasin or Banjo commission, the general recommendation was the same - the need for government to control education at the state and federal levels (Amadi, 1979, p. 532). These commissions also recommended that education should be tailored to meet the needs of Nigeria in particular and Africa in general. To identify the areas of need, a National Curriculum Conference was held at Ibadan in 1969 under the auspices of the Nigerian Education Research Council. The areas of need identified at this conference include: teacher education program, selection of text books for Nigerian schools, the beginning age for primary schools and the length of primary and secondary school programs.

The East Central State Education Edict, 1970

Shortly after the end of the Nigerian Civil War, the East Central State government passed the East Central State Education Edict, 1970, whose objective was to see to it that:

> The schools in the State become functional within the shortest possible time after the vast destruction and damage suffered by existing schools in the course of the Civil War.
>
> It is desirable and necessary that the state takes over all schools within the state and their control, management, and supervision in order to secure central control and an integrated system of education which will guarantee uniform standards and fair distribution of educational facilities and reduce the cost of running the schools.
>
> The take-over will ensure that schools which are in effect financed by the people and managed by their accredited representatives will more readily provide stability, satisfy the people's basic educational and national needs, combat sectionalism, religious conflicts and disloyalty to the cause of a united Nigeria. (p. 1)

By this edict, the East Central State government assumed total and complete control and responsibility for education in the State. The East Central State example was soon followed by the other two Eastern states and indeed by nearly all the states in the federation except Plateau where in actual fact the government ran the schools by paying teachers' salaries, passing education ordinances and determining the school curriculum but working under the auspices of the missions. The East Central State, according to Amadi (1979),

> came forth with an innovative system which included pilot components never before used in any educational system in Nigeria or, perhaps, in Africa. It was revolutionary in scope, timing, and in the decision-making process. For the first time, the state assumed the primary and total responsibility for the education of its youths. (p. 533)

Starting with the East-Central State Edict[14] of 1970, the different state governments in Nigeria began a systematic take-over of schools from missions and voluntary agencies. Although this act took some parts of the nation by storm and raised a lot of dust (Afigbo, 1968, p. 176), debate on government active participation in education was by no means new among Nigerian educated elites.

In 1900, Henry Rawlinson Carr (hereafter Henry Carr)[15], for instance, wrote:

> ...The aim of the missionary societies in establishing schools is entirely different from that of the government or practical men. The missionaries look upon schools as instruments for making converts, other men view them as instruments for making good and useful citizens. (Taiwo, 1975, p. 50)

In his annual report of 1902, Henry Carr again advocated:

> If public education is to make any progress commensurate with the general advancement of the Colony, it will be necessary for the Government and the Board of Education to firmly make up their minds as to what objects the schools are to subserve and to the best means of attaining those objects. A really suitable and efficient system of education--which ought for this country to be both literary and manual --cannot be cheap. Such a mode of education cannot be provided under a voluntary system. It is to the Government and not to the people themselves that we should under existing circumstances look for the perfecting of what is nothing less than a political instrument of the highest value. (Taiwo, 1975, p. 39)

And in a keynote address to the Diocesan Synod session of 1902, Henry Carr reemphasized his call for government active participation in education as follows:

> Let it be remembered that the promotion of education, although it is a matter of public concern, yet is more nearly a matter of national concern. The education of the people is the interest of the Government, but it is also the debt which the old owes to the new generation... (Taiwo, 1975, p. 39)

Indeed, even the colonial government in Nigeria wanted to have some measure of control over education at least as a means of social control. Hence, in spite of its fragile administration and meagre resources, the colonial government passed an ordinance in 1882 which authorized the appointment of an Inspector of Education for all the British West African settlements including Lagos. The same ordinance established certain criteria for grants-in-aid based on organization, discipline, excellence, subjects offered, attendance and percentage passes. Another reason for the desire to control education was that the colonial government was particularly unhappy with the missions for teaching equality of mankind. Lord Lugard, the first Governor-General of Nigeria made his views and indeed the view of the entire colonial administration known on this subject when he wrote this about the African Evangelical Mission in 1906:

> I regret to say that I do not have very good reports of this mission from any of their stations. I am informed that they preach the equality of Europeans and natives, which, however true from a doctrinal point of view, is apt to be misapplied by the people in a low stage of development, and interpreted as an abolition of class distinction. (Taiwo, 1975, p. 79)

In the *Dual Mandate*, Lugard outlined the type of education he would like to see for Africans as follows:

> (Education) should train a generation able to achieve ideals of its own, without a slavish imitation of Europeans, capable and willing to assume its own definite sphere of public and civic work, and to shape its own future. The education afforded to that section of the population who intend to lead the lives which their forefathers led should enlarge their outlook, increase their efficiency and standard of comfort, and bring them into closer sympathy with the Government, instead of making them unsuited to and ill-contented with their mode of life. (Lugard, 1922/1965, pp. 425-426)

With respect to the education of the sons of traditional rulers Lugard had this to say:

> The diffusion of education throughout the country, and especially the education of the sons of native rulers, is particularly desirable in order to avoid the present danger of a separate educated class... in rivalry with the accepted rulers of the people. (Lugard, 1922/1965, p. 426)

From the 1920s, the colonial government was the more upset with the missions because they were engaged in what was called literary education which flooded the streets with educated but unemployed and unemployable Nigerians--a cause of much social and political unrest (Afigbo, 1978, p. 179). In the Annual Report for the

Southern Provinces of Nigeria, the government was forthright in its condemnation of mission education. The report noted:

> Much of the discontent and many of the social problems of present times in Nigeria...can be identified with a system of education which was, and in a measure still is, foreign to the lives of the people, and which formulated without true perspective and, being alike for rural and urban areas, caters for neither. (Afigbo, 1978, p. 188)

In that same year (1921) Lugard summed up the government's position on primary and secondary school education in the following words:

> The chief function of Government primary and secondary schools among primitive communities is to train the more promising boys from the village schools as teachers for those schools, as clerks for the local native courts, and as interpreters. (Nduka, 1965, p. 21)

And the 1925 colonial memorandum titled "Education Policy in British Tropical Africa" stated:

> Education should be adapted to the mentality, aptitudes, occupations and traditions of the various peoples; care must be taken to avoid creating a hiatus between the educated class and the rest of the community. (Nduka, 1965, p. 43)

But Afigbo (1978) argues that:

> In spite of its brawls with the missions and mission schools over education, the colonial government had never evolved more than a basically conservative educational policy. True it wanted an educational system fitted to indigenous society, but this was not for the purpose of changing the inner springs of society, nor for bringing about a social, economic and political revolution, but for keeping indigenous society in its traditional groove. (p. 181)

For whatever pretensions, however, starting from 1882, the colonial government not only subsidized mission education in Nigeria but drew up guidelines to be followed by missions to qualify for grants-in-aid. Following this, the government set up an inspectorate division in 1899 to monitor the guidelines for grants, for as the saying goes, "he who pays the piper dictates the tune." In the next instance, the government arrogated to itself the authority to close down schools that did not meet its so-called standards. And Afigbo (1978) notes: "...it would appear that the colonial authority would have preferred, if it had the capacity in terms of money and personnel, to take over full responsibility for education in the territory" (p. 178).

In the late 1950s, however, the advent of nationalist governments ushered in increased debate on church participation in education in Nigeria. After all, Nigerians were equally unhappy with Christian education. For example, Nigerians were unhappy with the literary curriculum of the Christian mission schools which did not place sufficient emphasis on science, technology and agriculture--the last of which was the mainstay of the nation's economy. On this note the participants at the conference on the Review of the Educational System of Eastern Nigeria expressed their misgivings with mission education as follows:

> ...the colonial type of education...did not adequately meet the needs of the country... The result is that manual, agricultural and technical education have come to be associated with inferior status and to be accorded low instead of high regard in the scheme of things. (Afigbo, 1978, p. 182)

Also appalling to the nationalist governments was the unnecessary duplication of schools, programs and facilities in particular areas to the neglect of others, occasioned by rivalries between missions. These rivalries were sometimes replicated in the communities as well. Abernethy (1969) reports such unhealthy rivalries between communities in Igboland as follows:

> Traditional rivalries...were reinforced by denominational rivalries, and the reinforcement often had the effect of weakening or even destroying the village's sense of identity. The rivalry in Owerri Province, where in many areas Catholics had arrived first, followed a somewhat different pattern. A village with a Roman Catholic Mission (R.C.M.) school or church would be "presumed lost" by the Church Missionary Society...The Catholics in their turn would bypass the C.M.S. village and open a station in some neighboring area. Thus Orlu and Emekuku soon became known as Catholic towns, whereas Nkwerre was generally considered an Anglican stronghold. When an influential chief was converted to one faith or the other, he sometimes

>discouraged other Christian groups from entering his territory. (pp. 46-47)

Indeed apart from unhealthy rivalries prompted by competing missions, proliferation of schools increased the cost of grants for the state governments. It was as a result of the huge sum required for grants that even the colonial government made the supervision of schools mandatory and the condition for grants-in-aid more vigorous. On their own part, the nationalists thought that the only way of eliminating indiscriminate establishment of schools was by putting the missions out of the business of education entirely since schools had become unfortunate avenues for conversion and rivalry. Also attracting the criticism of the nationalists was the utter disrespect shown to African culture by Christian mission education in preference for Western cultural values. As in the earlier case, the participants in the Report on the Review of Education in Eastern Nigeria were very vocal in their condemnation of the existing order and called for reform thus:

> the present political and social status of Nigeria demands a reorganization of the existing educational system which would better reflect our spiritual, moral and cultural values and at the same time meet the challenge of the growing needs of the nation. (Afigbo, 1978, p. 185)

Given these anomalies, in the considered view of the nationalists, the simplest answer to missions' "menace" was to put them completely out of the business of education, for although mission domination of public education had been tolerated, it was not considered good enough for the nation. Afigbo (1978) however, argues that:

> ...it would be misleading to think it was just dissatisfaction with the actual performance of the missions in the field (of education) that exposed them to the unrelenting attack from the nationalists. (p. 186)

According to him, the nationalists saw missionaries as collaborators who through the kind of education they offered to Africans had helped in promoting the stability of the colonial regime. Besides, the nationalists believed that colonialism had grips not only on the body politic but also on the economy and the educational system as well. The state control of education, the nationalists reasoned, would produce the type of citizens needed in the new nation state. This nationalist position will be appreciated if we understand that missionaries and colonial administrators were birds of the same feather who flocked together in many occasions. Indeed, Ayandele (1967) maintains that "(in Nigeria) missionary propaganda from its inception was inextricably bound up with political consideration" (p. 5). "From the start", he adds, "...missionary propaganda in Nigeria was not just a religious invasion. In effect it was associated with a political invasion as well" (p. 8). Abernethy (1969) corroborates Ayandele's assertion when he states:

> Although it would be an oversimplification to describe them as advance agents of British (or French) imperialism, the missionaries were linked in many ways to the traders and officials who came in increasing numbers to Nigeria. (p. 32)

Both contentions are confirmed by Professor Du Plessis who, in 1929 wrote:

> Missionary enterprise is so intimately related to the political movement on the one hand and to the commercial undertaking on the other, that its history cannot be accurately traced without continued reference to both. (cited in Ekechi, 1972, p. 1)

It is therefore not an overstatement when Ayandele (1969) describes missionaries as pathfinders to European rule in West Africa, for according to him, not only did missionaries prepare the way for the colonialist but they facilitated peaceful occupation by the colonial forces.

As a step towards the eventual takeover of schools from the missions and voluntary agencies in Nigeria, the different state governments set up commissions to review their educational programs and to advise the governments. It is therefore no surprise that Dr. S. E. Imoke, Minister of Education in Eastern Nigeria, spoke the minds of many educated Nigerians. In addressing one of such commissions he said:

> In quest for the right solution we have commissioned many experts to study and advise. Generally, such commissions have been manned

by non-Nigerians. The findings and recommendations of those commissions have been extremely helpful to us... But no foreigner, no matter how sincere, knowledgeable and objective can see or feel our problems in exactly the same way as we ourselves; for they are bound to be influenced by circumstances and conditions which, while relevant in their own countries and conditions may not be quite applicable to our set of circumstances and conditions. (Afigbo, 1978, p. 187)

Ten years after independence, therefore, the different state governments in Nigeria began to take over mission schools. What was the missions' attitude to government take-over of their schools? Missions' reaction to government take-over bid was sharp, swift, and uncompromising, particularly among Roman Catholics. As early as 1951, Archbishop David Mathew[16] had warned Catholic Bishops in Nigeria against developments in the Gold Coast (now Ghana) and Northern Rhodesia (now Zimbabwe) where proposals were being made for the eventual take-over of mission schools by their various governments (Cooke, 1978, p. 194). In a report to the Advisory Committee on Education in the Colonies, Archbishop Mathew emphasized the right of parents to choose the type of school best suited for their children's education and warned:

> I look on a Catholic school or a Moslem school as something rooted in the African scene. Our increasing number of family units have a right to a Catholic school for their children, and the African parent of any religious affiliation has the right to send his children to the type of school of his choice. (Cooke, 1978, p. 195)

In 1953, the Nigerian Catholic Bishops issued "The Joint Bishops' Circular on Education" in which they reiterated, among other things, "the prior rights of the family as regards the Christian education of its offspring and consequently also to respect the supernatural rights of the Church in the same realm of Christian education" (Cooke, 1978, p. 196).

During and after the take-over, the missions were locked in several and at times bitter court battles with the state governments for the return of their schools. In every case, however, the state governments won. This was in part due to the realization by Nigerian judges of the utmost importance of education as an indispensable agent of social change and progress which cannot be left to the whims and caprices of religious dictates.

Reasons for Government Take-Over of Schools in Nigeria

At this juncture it is important to examine the reasons why the state governments took over schools from the missions in Nigeria ten years after independence.

Education as a Fundamental Human Right

Following the Universal Declaration of Human Rights adopted by the United Nations General Assembly in December 1948, which asserts the right of individuals to education, most proponents of government take-over of schools in Nigeria (Fafunwa, 1971; Nwagwu, 1978; Fawehinmi, 1974), based their argument on it. The United Nations Declaration guarantees for the individual certain rights and freedoms as well as stipulates responsibilities. Article 26 of the Declaration asserts that:

> (1) Everyone has the right to education. Education shall be free, at least in the elementary and fundamental stages. Elementary education shall be compulsory. Technical and professional education shall be made generally available and higher education shall be equally accessible to all on the basis of merit... Parents have a prior right to choose the kind of education that shall be given to their children.

Most proponents of education as a fundamental human right argued that every Nigerian has a right to education, following the United Nations Declaration. They asserted that most Nigerians are denied a right to education purely on account of parental poverty which is just an accident of birth. If education is a human right, they argued, then no one should be denied equal access to education on account of parental financial position. In order to ameliorate the situation in a poor country like Nigeria, they maintained, government should take over the control and management of schools to enhance equal access by all.

Education as a Means of Political Socialization, Social and Economic Development

Abernethy (1969) and Uchendu, (1979) argue that politics plays and continues to play an important role in education decision-making. Proponents of this point of view in Nigeria, for example, maintained that Government should nationalize all sectors of formal education because: "any modern state has the manifest right and duty to look after the interests of its citizens - as it conceives and interprets these interests" (Okoh, 1983, p. 58).

Besides, education as a major political, social and economic tool serving such functions as political socialization, economic management and social direction, should be in the hands of the government. Indeed, as a key for forging national consciousness education should never be left in the hands of foreigners because foreign interest could not redress such issues of national concern as educational imbalance between the different parts of the country and the protection and transmission of the peoples' cultural heritage. It was also pointed out that after independence Nigeria needed an educational system that was socially relevant, that would forge her true confident and self-reliant identity. Such an education, it was believed, could not be left in the reign of free market forces since such forces could not serve communal/social national needs. And because the cost of education was so high, it could not be adequately provided by private enterprise. Finally, if we imagine for a moment that Nigeria spends about 30-40 per cent of her gross national product on education alone, it was only wise for such resources to be channeled appropriately in order to achieve the desired national objectives.

Drawing largely from the work of Paulo Freire (1970) Madike (1983) made a passionate case for government intervention in education. He argued that opposition to government take-over of schools in Nigeria stemmed from the fact that education was one sure way in which individuals in society were assigned positions of power, esteem, rank and wealth. Through the control of education, therefore, some people had imposed a "culture of silence" on the masses, thereby keeping the people perpetually "alienated" and in "a position of marginality." People in a position of marginality are defined as "people in a position of hunger, disease, despair, mental deficiencies, pain, promiscuity, and the impossibility of being" (cited in Madike, 1983, p. 52).

Like Carnoy (1974), and to some extent Bourdieu (1973, 1977), Madike (1983) maintained that education, particularly colonial education, existed to perpetuate the existing order; that it transmitted privileges, allocated status and instilled respect for the existing order. Though established to transmit knowledge, missionary education had contributed to the perpetuation of status cleavages. And like Bourdieu he argued that modern democracies rely on indirect coercion and resort to less direct physical violence to assure social control. The widespread belief in equality makes it difficult for the ruling class to grant ascriptive status overtly. Hence, new and more discrete means must be found. This role was assigned to education under private control. In this way, minority upper class interest was preserved without violating democratic principles. Madike (1983) wrote:

> Many educated Nigerians share Freire's anxieties that the schools we inherited from our colonial masters contain attempts to silence, to rationalize the irrational, and to gain acceptance for structures that are oppressive. This type of colonialization, for this is what precisely it is, does not require imperialism, since it is possible for one class of the citizens of a country to colonize others. For example, it is possible for men to colonize women, whites to colonize blacks, a dominant ethnic group to colonize others, all within the same country. A colonized individual accepts readily the economic exploitation or cultural domination by the colonizer. These fears, while real, need to be verified with adequate, empirical evidence, and the situation corrected, if a country like Nigeria is to taste the fruits of stability. (pp. 52-53)

How does education perform this feat? Freire (1970) argues that the elites use education as a means of domination by encouraging the use of narrative learning "to make the majority adapt to the purpose the minority prescribe for them, thereby depriving them of the right to their own purpose" (cited in Madike, 1983, p. 53).

Madike prescribed problem posing education under government control as the only method of liberating the masses.

Educational Imbalance between the North and the South

The history of educational imbalance in Nigeria is traceable to the activities of the Christian missions. Realizing the futility of trying to convert men of good standing in society, the Christian missions turned their attention to the youths and schools in the hope that they would "win the people through the children and the children through the schools" (Bray, 1981, p. 16). As schools became handmaids of evangelization, there was proliferation of schools in Southern Nigeria. In the north, partly because Christian missions started off late and largely because of British official policy of restricting Christian missions to non-Muslim areas, the work of the missions and indeed Western education was painfully slow because the colonial government took no initiative in the establishment of schools in the north until 1910, almost half a century after the first schools had been established in the south. Indeed, it was not until 1896 that the first school was ever established in any part of Northern Nigeria and the first missionaries to Kano settled there in 1894, half a century after they had established schools at Badagry in Southern Nigeria. As Christianity is a religion of the book, every good Christian must be able to read in order to recite his catechism, sing his hymns and read his Bible, as such education is necessary. Abernethy (1969) sums it up thus; "Christianity is a religion of the book... It was not sufficient for a preacher or a priest merely to proclaim the Gospel; his congregation must literally see the World (sic) as well as hear it" (p. 31). Certainly, there was a clear and distinct need for education and each mission established schools as soon as its initial grounds were cleared. Indeed, as Father M. Wauters pointed out, they knew the best way to make conversions was to open schools. Therefore when the district of Ekiti-Ondo was opened, they started schools before there was any church or mission house. For cultural and religious reasons, parents in the north resisted sending their children, particularly girls, to school even when such schools existed.

For one thing, northerners believed that Western education was an agent of Christianity. The next hindrance to the acceptance of Western education in Northern Nigeria was the purdah or practice of keeping women in seclusion after marriage. Finally, the existence of a well organized system of Muslim education in the north made the acceptance of Western education difficult. These factors, together with Lugard's pledge of 1903 barring missionary interference in Muslim areas of the north, created serious educational imbalance between the south and the north and within the north itself. Tables 9 and 10 show the educational disparity between the north and the south.

Table 9

Educational Development, Northern and Southern Nigeria

Year	Primary Schools North	Primary Schools South	Primary Enrollments North	Primary Enrollments South	Secondary Schools North	Secondary Schools South	Secondary Enrollments North	Secondary Enrollments South
1906	1	126	na	11,872	0	11	0	20
1912	34	150	954	35,716	0	13	0	67
1926	125	3,828	5,210	138,249	0	18	0	518
1937	549	3,533	20,269	218,610	1	26	65	4,285
1947	1,110	4,984	70,962	538,391	3	43	251	9,657
1957	1,080	13,473	185,484	2,343,317	18	176	3,643	28,208
1965	2,743	12,234	492,829	2,419,913	77	1,305	15,276	180,907
1972	4,225	10,313	854,466	3,536,731	255	964	63,515	337,288

Source: Bray, 1981, p. 17

Another cause for the educational imbalance between the north and the south was that, after the attainment of self government in the 1950s, the two southern governments embarked on unprecedented student enrollment through the Universal primary education scheme while the north concentrated on adult education.

Table 10

Primary Enrollments by Sex

	NORTH				SOUTH			
	BOYS		GIRLS		BOYS		GIRLS	
Year	No.	%	No.	%	No.	%	No.	%
1937	18,810	81.8	4,180	18.2	216,979	84.3	40,555	15.7
1955	129,523	76.8	38,998	23.2	1,024,031	68.7	465,644	31.3
1961	230,500	72.8	85,764	27.2	1,509,868	60.7	977,704	39.3
1966	367,776	70.8	151,088	29.2	1,477,591	58.9	1,029,526	41.1
1972	602,229	70.4	252,237	29.6	2,072,637	58.6	1,464,094	41.4

Source: Bray, 1981, p. 19

Hence, whereas before 1966, power in Nigeria resided in Sokoto, only about one in every 20 children of school age attended school in that province (*West Africa*, 1970, July, p. 798). Indeed, less than five percent of children of school age went to school in Sokoto. Whereas Lagos State had a primary school population of about 200,000 by 1972. This was by far larger than the enrollment in the six northern states in 1972. Despite the great efforts made by Kano State with respect to education, it was not expected that more than 15 per cent of the children of school age would be in school by 1975 (*West Africa*, 1972, p. 437).

Educational imbalance in Nigeria was not only horizontal, it was vertical as well; that is, between urban and rural areas of the same state; within the states themselves and between the different northern states. For instance, the 1968 education statistics show that while there were about 100,000 boys in primary schools in the two northern states of Benue and Plateau with a population of about 4 million people, there were fewer than that number of pupils in the former North-Western State with a total population of 5 ½ million. In secondary education, while there were over 4,570 boys in secondary grammar schools in Kwara State, there were just about that number in the two northern states of Benue and Plateau. And Kano with a population of over 6 million had student enrollment of 36,000 boys, 13,500 girls in primary schools and 1,300 boys, 570 girls in secondary schools in the State by 1968. During this period, there were over 700,000 pupils in primary schools,

60,000 in secondary schools, 22,000 in secondary modern schools in the West. In Lagos State alone, there were 207,000 children in primary schools by 1968. This number exceeds the total student enrollment for the former North-Western, North-Central and Kano States put together (*West Africa*, 1970, July, p. 798).

The educational imbalance between the north and the south was so serious that in a keynote address at the Conference of the National Council on Education, Chief Abdul Eke, Federal Commissioner for Education, said:

> From the national standpoint, however, the grossest and most alarming imbalance is to be seen in the very wide gap existing between the six Northern states on the one hand, and the six Southern states on the other hand... So wide is the gap...that for every child in primary school in the Northern states there are four in the Southern states, for every boy or girl in a secondary school in the north there are five in the south, and for every student in a post-secondary institution in the north there are six in the south. (*West Africa*, 1973, p. 37)

As a matter of fact, the situation of higher education was even more disquieting. It was for this reason that a quota system of appointment into the federal public service was suggested. However, this suggestion was rejected by the Chairman of the Federal Public Service Commission, himself a northerner, when he said:

> Some people in the states are asking for such a system, under which each state would have an equal, or proportionate to its population, share in federal jobs at all levels. Careful attention will have to be paid to this point of view in many very senior appointments; but the most cursory glance at the education statistics shows that for a great majority of federal appointments, particularly because of the ever increasing demands of the states' own services, it cannot possibly be met. (*West Africa*, 1970, July, p. 798)

Table 11

University of Ibadan Output - 1948-1966

Ibos	1,874
Yoruba	2,706
Edo	395
Urhobo	138
Hausa	31
Fulani	17
Tiv	6

Source: Adamu, 1973, p. 52

Another suggestion for redressing the educational imbalance between the north and the south was a quota system of admission into federally controlled universities and other institutions of learning. On this Adamu (1973), another northerner, wrote:

> The problem of equalizing educational opportunities for both the North as well as the Southern parts of the country cannot be solved by the introduction of the quota system alone. The quota system to be employed in the admission of students to federally owned institutions of higher learning, while desirable, cannot provide the solution to a problem which has already reached a crisis proportion. (Adamu, 1973, p. 70)

As a solution to the problem, Adamu (1973) suggested:

> What is needed, in my view, is a comprehensive regional educational policy. By region, I do not mean the Northern or the Southern region. I mean that Nigeria should be divided into educational regions or Training institutions. The Federal Ministry of Education should be involved not only in the formulation of the educational plans of these areas but should also be actively involved in its implementation, thereby making sure that the money provided is spent for the purpose for which it was allocated. This scheme, if adopted, will speed up the educational progress of the educationally under-developed areas without unduly retarding the normal rate of progress of the educationally advanced zones. (p. 71)

The most noteworthy suggestion for redressing the educational imbalance in Nigeria was given by General Yakubu Gowon, Nigeria Head of State 1966-1975.

Speaking at the 10th anniversary celebrations of the Ahmadu Bello University in Zaria, General Gowon addressed the issue of educational imbalance in Nigeria in the following words:

> An educational structure which is to be of lasting permanence and which aims at preventing future sectional imbalance must have a base which is broad enough and, indeed, coterminous with the entire population of the country...I believe that the basic and most important solution to the question of educational imbalance in the country must be found at the primary school level and our energies must be geared towards increasing, throughout the federation, especially in the educationally backward areas, the primary school population progressively until primary school education becomes free and compulsory for all the children in Nigeria. Once this is achieved...a firm foundation would have been laid for progressive universal free secondary education...university education will be available and be placed within the reach of all children who can profit by it. (*West Africa*, 1973, p. 37)

Educational Imbalance and the Nigerian Civil War

In Nigeria, a major source of friction between the north and the south is competition for official federal government jobs and resources which is a direct result of the differential in educational attainment between the two regions (Abernethy, 1969, pp. 263-268). While northerners believe that southerners have a monopoly of federal government appointments, southerners think that northerners are given federal government jobs out of political patronage and not based on qualification. It must be said that educational disparity between the north and the south translates proportionately to economic disparity between the two regions because according to Diejomaoh (1972):

> an examination of partial economic indices, such as per capita levels of human resource development, government expenditures and revenues, provision of health and transport facilities, and export levels, show quite clearly the differential in per capita income levels between the North and South. While per capita income differentials are traceable to a large number of factors, differentials in the level of modern educational attainment between the North and the South are largely responsible for the differentials in per capita incomes of

Northern and Southern Nigeria. (pp. 318-320)

Indeed, in 1966, for instance, of the 1333 students in Nigerian Universities only 83 were from the north. And as late as 1954, only one northerner possessed a University degree (Callaway, 1987, p. 134).

Table 12

University Population by Regions - 1966

Universities	North	East	West	Midwest	Lagos
Ahmadu Bello	74	38	18	10	2
Nsukka	2	395	54	72	6
Ibadan	4	166	204	27	2
Ife	2	61	130	24	-
Lagos	1	15	13	13	-
TOTAL	83	675	419	146	10

Source: Diejomaoh, 1972, p. 325

As a result of the uneven educational attainment in the country, southerners dominated the federal public service, federal corporations, and parastatals, federal universities and even industries. Notice how Adamu (1973) made this point:

> On balance, the results of the Universal Primary Education Scheme produced significantly large numbers of trainable resources (a small percentage of the output went to post primary institutions), to be trained as mechanics, plumbers and electricians. Since both the Eastern and Western governments could absorb only so much, those who were not employed by these governments, found their way to the Federal establishments, Northern Region Government service and into the private sector. (p. 50)

Southern domination of the federal services was to the utmost displeasure of northerners. This is how Sir Ahmadu Bello, the Sardauna of Sokoto, articulated northern fear that the country's administrative power would pass to southerners if self-government were granted in 1956. This is the Sardauna's poignant pronouncement:

As things were at that time [the early 1950s], if the gates to the departments were to be opened, the Southern Regions had a huge pool from which they could find suitable people, while we had hardly anyone. In the resulting scramble it would, we were convinced, be inevitable that the Southern applicants would get almost all the posts available. Once you get a Government post you are hard indeed to shift...[This] was a matter of life and death to us ...If the British Administration had failed to give us the even development that we deserved and for which we craved so much-and they were on the whole a very fair administration-what had we to hope from an African Administration, probably in the hands of a hostile party. The answer to our minds was, quite simply, just nothing, beyond a little window dressing. (Abernethy, 1969, p. 264)

Education and Integration

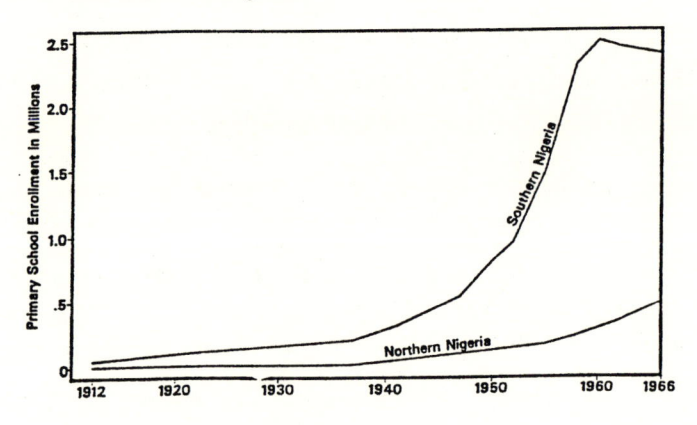

Figure 1 Primary School Enrollment, 1912-65

Source: Abernethy, 1969, p. 263

Education and Integration

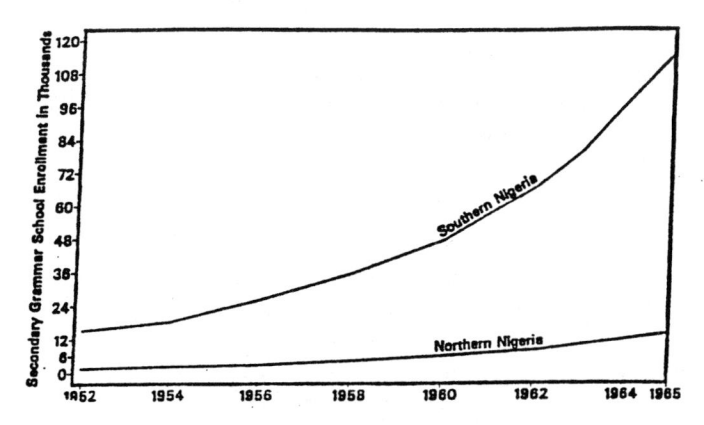

Figure 2. Secondary Grammar School Enrollment, 1952-65

Source: Abernethy, 1969, p. 265

But while southerners dominated the public service, northerners through their numerical strength controlled the political scene in Nigeria. Another source of considerable dissatisfaction among southerners was the imposition of some less qualified northerners on them. This state of affairs led to the military coup of 1966 in Nigeria which was organized predominantly by Ibo officers. This was the coup which brought Major-General J. T. U. Aguiyi-Ironsi, an Ibo officer, to power.

While dissatisfaction between the north and south was responsible for the military coup of 1966, education differential between the north and south was responsible for the failure of Decree Number 34 promulgated by General Ironsi which attempted to establish a unitary government in Nigeria. The greatest fear of the north was that through Decree Number 34 the south will dominate not only the federal public service as they had done but they will also dominate the northern public service as well if jobs were given out according to qualification. An article in the *New Nigerian* of August 22, 1966 enunciated northern fears of southern domination as exemplified by decree number 34. Part of the article which was written by Abubakar Tuggar reads as follows:

> The appointment of various study groups to examine ways and means of unifying the country into one solid whole, the declared intention of the former Military Government later to abolish the Regions, and the issuing, haphazardly, of decrees that took the form of extreme centralization were signs of things to come. But the proclamation of decree No. 34 which transformed Nigeria into a unitary state overnight seemed to be the last straw which broke the camel's back...What mattered to the former Military Government was the selfish ambition of some tribesmen to dominate the whole country by all means, fair or foul...As a master plan continued to unfold itself we saw being undertaken mass recruitment into the army-with the long arm of tribalism playing its full part, of course-to precede the appointment of Military Prefects and provincial Military Courts so that the former Military Government would be able to take its administration from the national down to the village level. Thus a reign of terror, having been created, was to be perpetuated. (Akpan, 1971, p. 29)

It was this state of affairs which led to the counter coup organized by northern officers which overthrew General Aguiyi-Ironsi, a southerner, and replaced him with Lt. Col. Yakubu Gowon, later General Gowon, a northerner in July, 1966. Thereafter a series of killings and massacres were perpetrated against southerners, particularly the Ibos, between September and October 1966. Diejomaoh (1972) maintains that:

> The communal riots in the North in September and October of 1966, in which numerous Ibos as well as other Southerners such as Yorubas, Edos, and Efiks were killed and forced to flee the North, were a reaction of Northerners against economic domination by Southerners. These Southerners were able to entrench themselves in a dominating position in the North largely by dint of their relatively higher levels of educational attainment. (p. 321)

Indeed, Diejomaoh argues that the fear of domination was so great that the northern officers who organized the counter coup wanted to take the Northern Region out of the Nigerian Federation despite the serious economic consequences that would have followed such an action.

The level of educational attainment therefore was related to the Nigerian crisis and missionaries were indirectly responsible for the crisis in that they created the imbalance and the education differential which precipitated the crisis. Education was related to the crisis in another way. At the beginning of confrontations, it was thought that since the Ibos were so highly educated and were employed at every level of the Nigerian economy, their departure to the East would lead to the collapse of the Nigerian economy. This did not turn out to be so because other educated Nigerians, particularly the Yorubas and a few Hausas, rose to the occasion by filling the vacuum created by the departing Ibos.

Education as an Investment

An important reason for government take-over of schools in Nigeria was the desire to use education as an investment in human capital, for ten years after independence no efforts were made to refashion education to meet Nigeria's needs. Indeed, until the East Central State Education Edict of 1970, formal education in Nigeria was largely in the hands of Christian missions resulting in an unplanned and uncoordinated educational system. The result being that in most instances, people with skills irrelevant to the needs of Nigeria were produced. By the 1970s, most state governments in Nigeria had come to realize that what Nigeria needed was:

> a system of education that is distinctively Nigerian and tailored to meet the needs of the present development decade and to lay the basis for the achievement of a big-power status in the not too distant future. (*West Africa*, 1973, January, p. 37)

Proponents of education as an investment were divided into two camps. Those in the first camp believed that "education should be provided for its own sake, as a consumer good and a means of enriching an individual's knowledge and developing his/her full personality" (*West Africa*, 1973, January, p. 37). In the second camp were those who believed that education is "a capital good; that it should seek to prepare people to undertake specific tasks and employment functions which are essential for the transformation of their environment" (*West Africa*, 1973, January, p. 37). It was perhaps on the latter perspective that the Ashby Commission, officially referred to as, *Commission on Post-School Certificate and Higher Education in Nigeria*, was appointed by the then Federal Minister for Education in April, 1959. The Commission had as its term of reference "to conduct an investigation into Nigeria's need in the field of post-school Certificate and Higher Education over the next twenty years" (Asiwaju, 1972, p. 2). The Commission Report entitled *Investment in Education*, acknowledged that Nigeria in the 1970s will be:

> A nation of some fifty million people, with industries, oil, and well developed agriculture; intimately associated with other free African countries...a voice to be listened to (in the world); with its traditions in art preserved and fostered and with the beginnings of its own literature, a nation which is taking its place in a technological civilization... (Asiwaju, 1972, p. 4)

In order to meet the manpower needs of the nation in the 1970s, the Commission recommended that there should be about 80,000 Nigerians with post-secondary education. Out of this number, 30,000 will be needed in administration and the professions, of which at least 20,000 should be graduates of universities spread among the various disciplines - liberal arts, the social sciences, agriculture, the physical and biological sciences, medicine, engineering and law. The various disciplines were to be related to local needs however. The report also envisioned that:

> Millions of people who will live in this Nigeria of 1980 are already born. Under the present educational system more than half of them will never go to school... Somehow, before 1980, as many talented children as possible must be discovered and educated... This is a stupendous undertaking. It will cost large sums of money. The Nigerian people will have to forgo other things they want so that every available penny is invested in education. Even this will not be enough. (Bray, 1981, p. 23)

Gani Fawehinmi (1974) also made the point that:

> In the developed world - United States of America, USSR, Britain, France, Japan...etc., education is seen as a profitable investment, contributing to economic growth. These countries have seen that education fulfills a double function - as a consumption good and as a production factor. So education becomes an integral part of economic and social development; schooling is considered a profitability, in fact, a strikingly valuable investment since it contributes to the wealth of the countries. (Fawehinmi, 1974, p. 26)

The idea of education as an investment was not new to Nigerian elites. Dr. Nnamdi Azikiwe, the most popular Nigerian politician, wrote this while he was still a student in the United States:

> I pray that the Lord may help me so that I may return to Africa with the golden fleece, and propagate from the Zambezi to the Nile, yea! from the Nile to the Congo, the new learning, the recent philosophy of education, that education itself is life and not necessarily a preparation for life. (Abernethy, 1969, p. 118)

Similarly, Chief Obafemi Awolowo, another Nigerian politician, stated in his autobiography as follows: "To educate the children and enlighten the illiterate adults is to lay a solid foundation not only for future social and economic progress but also for political stability" (Abernethy, 1969, p. 131). As an investment in the political future of the nation, Chief Awolowo added: "a truly educated citizenry is, in my view, one of the most powerful deterrents to dictatorship, oligarchy, and feudal autocracy" (Abernethy, 1969:131). From 1970 onwards, the different state governments in Nigeria began to take over schools from missions because they had come to realize that education was an investment which if properly utilized and harnessed would yield the expected results.

Disparity In Teachers' Conditions of Service

As we have seen, the establishment of schools, at least, in Southern Nigeria was the prerogative of Christian missions. However, the conditions of service for teachers in mission schools were different from those existing in the few government owned and operated schools. So also were conditions different in Native Authority and voluntary agency schools in the north. Until 1938, for instance, teachers in Native Authority schools in the north had no definite scales of salaries and had no increments. And until 1942 female teachers in mission schools were earning two-thirds the salary paid to their male counterparts with similar qualifications and experience (Onwuka, 1982, p. 146). Also, teachers with similar qualifications and experience earned different salaries depending on whether they were teaching in assisted or unassisted, mission or government schools. The most disturbing disparity existed between teachers in government schools and those in mission schools. While university graduates with teaching qualifications, for instance, earned £1584 within three years of their employment in government schools, it took a university graduate with the same qualifications and experience in a mission school fifteen years to get to that salary scale. Similarly, while a graduate teacher in a government school was entitled to a car advance for the purchase of his private car as soon as he joined the service, a graduate teacher in a mission school could only buy his car from his own savings. Disparity in teachers' conditions of service often led to friction and occasionally to strikes. There was the case of the teachers' strike of 1936 by teachers of the Church of Scotland Mission in Calabar and Creek Town. There was also the nationwide strike of 1964 by the Nigerian Union of Teachers, whose purpose was to press for better conditions of service for all Nigerian teachers. Another area of discomfort was the dual control of schools between the government and the Native Authorities on the one hand and missions on the other. It has indeed been documented that while about £1000 was used in the maintenance of a government primary school, a mission school with secondary classes received between £300 and £350 per annum (Onwuka, 1982, p. 132). Take the case of Denis Memorial Grammar School in Onitsha which

> ...had, on the staff, three Europeans (excluding one who was on leave), one African with a London University degree, two Yaba and two Achimota graduates, five certificated teachers - one holding the Senior Certificate - and two technical teachers. There were 330

students all of whom were boarders. Yet, the total government grant in the late 1930s for the school was £599. (Onwuka, 1982, pp. 132-133)

Disparity between the conditions of service in government operated and mission run schools was so glaring that members of the salary review commission known as the Adebo Commission appointed by the Federal Government of Nigeria in 1970 after the civil war to review the salaries and conditions of service of Nigerian workers commented as follows:

> Surely the time has come to do away with the cumbrous patchwork that is the Nigerian educational system at primary and secondary levels...(it) should be planned in a coherent, decisive manner and executed in an efficient, consistent fashion. The Christian, Moslem and other agencies did yeoman services for education in the past, for which the country will be forever grateful. They will be doing disservice to the national cause if they should stand in the way of a complete overhaul that will enable the Government to ASSUME COMPLETE RESPONSIBILITY FOR PLANNING, FINANCING AND RUNNING OF THE SCHOOLS. (*West Africa*, 1971, November, p. 1379, capitals added)

The Commissioners were forthright in their condemnation of the lackadaisical system of educational control in Nigeria. Releasing their venom on the dual system of education control in the country they said, "One of the consequences of the existing situation is an embarrassing disparity between teachers in government schools and those in non-government grant-aided schools" (*West Africa*, 1971, November, p. 1379). Calling for the complete take-over of schools by the state governments as the only solution to the existing disparity in the school system, the Commissioners maintained:

> As the Asabia Commission saw the situation, a complete integration of pay rates was impossible without the Government assuming propriety control of all the schools, with jurisdiction over the staffing arrangements. This Commission considers such integration to be a national necessity, recommends that it should be carried out, and recommends that the structural reforms that are undoubtedly a prerequisite of it should be accepted. (*West Africa*, 1971, November, p. 1379)

Systematically some state governments began to take over schools from missions in order to harmonize teachers' conditions of service, improve efficiency and halt drift by teachers, thereby enhancing the standard and quality of education in their states.

Religious Cleavages

Of some concern to the state governments was the issue of religious cleavages. In order to implant their own brand of religion, missionaries introduced cleavages along religious lines into Nigeria. Besides, "a 'good' citizen in Nigeria between 1860 and 1960," according to one writer, "meant one who was African by blood, Christian by religion, and British by culture. Others who were Moslems and traditionalists were only tolerated or accommodated" (Izuchi, 1986, p. 66). A major division existed between Christians and Muslims because in their attempt to win for themselves converts, Christian missions used books, sermons, hymns and schools. Indeed "the schools...were places where pupils went in as pagans and Muslims, and came out as converted Christians" (Fafunwa, 1974, p. 100). In order to prevent complete conversion of Muslims to Christianity, Muslims refused to send their children to Christian schools. Of grave concern to the Nigerian nation was the fact that schools were producing good Catholics, good Anglicans, good Methodists, good Baptists and good Muslims (in the case of the Muslim schools), and not good Nigerians. In the Eastern Regional elections of 1957 and 1961, bloc voting along religious lines was apparent. Indeed, due to the Roman Catholic policy of concentrating on primary school education, a situation arose in Eastern Nigeria where the mass of the population were Roman Catholics while the ruling elites were Protestants or saw things from a Protestant point of view because they had received part or all of their higher education in Protestant schools. To reduce religious tensions created by mission schools, some state governments decided to take over schools from missions.

CHAPTER VI

CONSEQUENCES OF GOVERNMENT TAKE-OVER OF SCHOOLS IN NIGERIA

With the takeover of schools, government began to harness the spirit of self-help of the various communities for the improvement of schools which hitherto had been lacking. Hence, communities began to participate in the running and management of their local schools through membership in Parent-Teacher-Associations (PTA), school committees, and divisional school boards. With the zonal redistribution of secondary schools, more students were able to attend schools, some from their homes rather than from boarding houses as was the case with mission schools. The reduction in fees was a great relief to parents and students alike. Indeed, as Amadi (1979) has argued, the zonal redistribution of secondary schools provided options to many more students, equal staffing, equipment and uniform standards. Admission on the basis of ethnicity and creed became a thing of the past. Also, government began to take more initiatives in education.

The Universal Free Primary Education

A major development in Nigerian education since 1970 was the introduction of the Universal Free Primary Education (UPE) in 1976. The Universal Free Primary Education scheme was designed as Nigeria's strategy for national development, national integration and nation-building (Clarke, 1978). As a policy program, it was hoped that the Universal Free Primary Education would bridge the educational gap between the north and the south and facilitate the development of an indigenous source of trained and skilled manpower for the construction and maintenance of Nigeria's development projects (Clarke, 1978). Indeed, according to the National Policy on Education "education is the greatest force that can be used to bring about redress, the greatest investment a nation can make for the quick development of its economic, political, sociological and human resources" (National Policy on Education, 1977). According to this policy, therefore, education is to be the key to Nigeria's development. However, it was also believed that there were certain groups who were unlikely to benefit from educational opportunities in Nigeria until the government abolished primary school fees, increased the teaching force and secularized the ownership of schools.

At the introduction of the UPE in 1976, primary school population in Nigeria jumped from 4,000,000 to 7,400,000. By 1980 this figure rose to 11,500,000 and stood at 14,000,000 by 1983. Also, in 1976, 3,600 additional primary school classrooms were built in Nigeria and 6,000 additional teachers were provided. In Northern Nigeria, the number of students attending primary, secondary and teacher training colleges has been phenomenal since 1976. In Bauchi state, for example, 300,000 elementary pupils were enrolled in schools in 1976 as opposed to 132,000 who enrolled in September of the previous year. In Sokoto state, 80,000 pupils enrolled in schools in 1976 representing a 40 percent increase. In the North East state, there were 300,000 pupils attending elementary schools in 1976 which was 43 percent above the 1968 figure (Clarke, 1978). There was even greater increase in the number of students attending secondary schools in the North East state because whereas there were only 3,400 students attending 19 secondary schools in 1968, there were 12,000 students attending 48 secondary schools in the state by 1976. Although the UPE program has been modified by some state governments because of lack of funds, it has stimulated considerable interest in primary education in Nigeria.

Table 13

Student Enrollment Trends in Primary and Secondary Schools

	Enrollment	
Date	**Primary**	**Secondary**
1960	2,912,618	135,364
1966	3,025,981	211,305
1973	4,746,808	448,909
1975-1980	11,521,500 (estimated)	1,555,180 (estimated)

Source: Aguolu, 1979, p. 526

Table 14

Trends in Student Enrollment in Nigerian Universities

Date	**Enrollment**
1959/60	1,113
1966/67	9,170
1973/74	23,814
1975/76	31,377

Source: Aguolu, 1979, p. 526

National Policy on Education

The framework for the National Policy on Education was laid by the Second National Development Plan, 1970-74. The Second National Development Plan recognized the educational imbalance between the north and the south of Nigeria as well as within the states themselves particularly regarding the availability of prerequisite expertise and skills and noted:

> While some states have a surfeit of some skills, others,..are experiencing shortage in similar fields. These have given rise to the persistent problems of educational gap among the different geographical areas of the country and the attendant issue of free mobility of skills from one part to any other part of the country. (Nigeria, Second National Development Plan, 1970-1974, p. 237).

The primary goal of the *Second National Development Plan*, 1970-1974, then was to eliminate inequity resulting from educational imbalance (Aguolu, 1979). The *Second National Development Plan*, 1970-1974, was designed to build:

    1) a united, strong and self-reliant nation;

    2) a great and dynamic economy;

    3) a just and egalitarian society;

    4) a land (which is) bright and full of opportunities for all its citizens; and

    5) a free and democratic society. (Aguolu, 1979)

The *Third National Development Plan,* 1975-1980, further emphasized the need to eradicate educational imbalance in Nigeria as a way of eliminating inequalities. The plan's first objective was "to expand facilities for education aimed at equalizing access to education throughout the country" (*Third National Development Plan*, 1975-1980, Vol. 1 p. 245). As can be seen, the national development plans set the stage for the National Policy on Education to follow because in these plans the federal government had made explicit its awareness of unequal distribution of educational facilities in the country. Even the First National Development Plan specifically cited as its main objective, "to develop as rapidly as possible opportunities in education, health, and employment, and to improve access for all citizens to these opportunities." The plan also aimed at achieving "a more equitable distribution in income both among people and among regions" (*National Development Plan*, 1962-68, p. 23). Some of the factors which were found to inhibit equal educational opportunities in Nigeria include: limited supply of schools; uneven diffusion of educational demand; differential impact of colonial rule; greater variation in the geographical spread of agencies of modernization such as schools, churches, and publishing houses; marked differences between urban and rural districts; and high school fees (Aguolu, 1979, p. 522). In order to solve ethnic tensions in Nigeria resulting from educational imbalance, the federal government issued the National Policy on Education in accordance with the Third National Development Plan, 1975-1980. Paragraph 14, page 244 reads:

consideration of justice and equity demand equalization of such opportunity as education such that every Nigerian child should have comparable opportunities for self-development and fulfillment irrespective of where he lives and the economic and social circumstances into which he was born.

The National Policy on Education was first introduced in 1977 and revised in 1981. A major objective of the national policy was to enhance a more and even distribution of income among individuals and socio-economic groups, because the Nigerian government had realized that the only solution to ethnic conflicts and tensions resulting from educational imbalance was to ensure equitable distribution of educational facilities and to narrow the gap between the more developed and less developed ethnic groups.

In its national policy on education, the Federal government of Nigeria affirmed that it had "adopted education as an instrument par excellence for effecting national development", having realized that the development of human resources is the key to a modernization process. Accordingly, through education Nigeria hopes to achieve:

> ...a free and democratic society; a just and egalitarian society; a united, strong and self-reliant nation; a great and dynamic economy; and a land of bright and full opportunities for all. (*National Policy on Education* 1977, 2)

The policy goes on to state that it is the responsibility of Nigerian education to achieve the following objectives:

- inculcate national consciousness and national unity;
- inculcate the right type of values and attitudes for the survival of the individual and the Nigerian society;
- train the mind in the understanding of the world around;
- acquire appropriate skills, abilities and competencies;
- that Nigeria should be a free, just and democratic society, a land full of opportunities for all citizens.

(*National Policy on Education* 1977, 3-5)

The National Policy on Education made two major policy changes in secondary school education in Nigeria. These are in the structure and the curriculum of secondary education. In the structure, the National Policy recommended substituting the five-year continuous secondary school program with a six year program to be given in two stages; the Junior Secondary School stage and the Senior Secondary School stage. Each stage would be of three years duration. For some students, the Junior Secondary School would mark the end of their formal education. But there is provision for those who wish to re-enter the system to do so later. The Junior Secondary School is to serve as a "career selection period." With regard to the curriculum, the National Policy recommended that the Junior Secondary School should be both pre-vocational and academic while the Senior Secondary School would run comprehensive programs incorporating technical and vocational subjects. By this policy, secondary school education which used to be mainly academic in its contents incorporated aspects of technical and vocational training.

National Values

The *National Policy on Education* set forth the moral tone for Nigerian education as follows:

(1) respect for the worth and dignity of the individual;
(2) faith in (people's) ability to make rational decisions;
(3) moral and spiritual values in inter-personal and human relations;
(4) shared responsibility for the common good of society;
(5) respect for the dignity of labor; and
(6) promotion of the emotional, physical and psychological health of all children. (National Policy on Education, 1981, p. 7)

How to Implement the Policy?

The *National Policy on Education* states the following on how to implement the national education policy:

(1) Education will continue to be highly rated in the national development plans, because education is the most important instrument of change as any fundamental change in the intellectual and social outlook of any society has to be preceded by an educational revolution;

(2) Lifelong education will be the basis for the nation's educational policies;

(3) Educational and training facilities will be multiplied and made more accessible, to afford the individual a far more diversified and flexible choice;

(4) Educational activity will be centered on the learner for maximum self-development and fulfillment;

(5) Universal basic education, in a variety of forms, depending on needs and possibilities, will be provided for all citizens;

(6) Efforts will be made to relate education to overall community needs;

(7) Educational assessment and evaluation will be liberalized by basing them in whole or in part on continuous assessment of the progress of the individual;

(8) Modern educational techniques will be increasingly used and improved at all levels of the education system;

(9) The educational systems will be structured to develop the practice of self-learning.

(10) At any stage of the educational process after primary education, an individual will be able to choose between continuing (one's) full-time studies, combining work with study, or embarking on full-time employment without excluding the prospect of resuming studies later on;

(11) Opportunity will continue to be made available for religious instruction. No child will be forced to accept any religious instruction which is contrary to the wishes of (the) parents; and

(12) Physical education will be emphasized at all levels of the educational system. (National Policy on Education, 1981, pp. 8-9)

Language

The National Policy acknowledged the importance of language in the nation's educative process but regretted the problems arising from implementing a lingua franca due to the multiplicity of ethnic groups and languages in Nigeria. The government, however, recommended that students should be encouraged to learn at least one of the three major languages in Nigeria (Hausa, Ibo and Yoruba) in addition to their mother tongue.

General Overview of the Policy

The policy set forth the aims and implementation procedures for all levels of education in Nigeria, details of which is not the primary concern of this book.

Consequences of Government Intervention in Education in Nigeria

Consequent upon government intervention and eventual take-over of schools from Christian missions, the number of students in Nigerian schools has risen dramatically. In 1983, there were 14 million pupils in primary schools in Nigeria as opposed to 4.7 million in 1973. Between 1975 and 1980, secondary school enrollment stood at 1.5 million but by 1983 the figure had risen to 3.6 million. By 1983 the opportunity for secondary school education in Nigeria had increased 2.4 times what it was in 1980 and 5 times what was available in 1976. Indeed, there was an increase of 2,881,937 students in Nigerian secondary schools between 1975 and 1983 (Kurian 1988).

The expansion of education in Northern Nigeria has been tremendous. In 1960 there were 2.913 million children in Nigerian primary schools out of which only 9.7 percent came from the north. In 1970 3.5 million children were enrolled in Nigerian primary schools 16.6 percent came from the north. In the 1980s student enrollment in the north increased to 38 percent in elementary schools and 26 percent in secondary schools. In the 1990s student enrollment in the north stands at about 40 percent in elementary schools and 30 percent in secondary schools (Iweriebor, 1996). Growth in university and other aspects of higher education has been equally impressive. Enrollment in universities in Nigeria increased from 338 in 1951 to 110,243 in 1985 and to 200,000 in 1996. In 1960, Nigeria inherited a national literacy rate of five percent but now the national literacy rate stands at 52 percent. In 1981, the Population Reference Bureau statistics showed that only six percent of adult women in Nigeria attained literacy, today about 42 percent of the adult women in Nigeria have attained literacy (Iweriebor, 1996). Indeed, women now constitute 40 percent of the national literate population in Nigeria. In real numbers, there are about 25 million literate women of all ages in Nigeria today (Iweriebor, 1996). With the introduction of the Universal Primary Education (UPE) in 1976, school fees were abolished in elementary schools in Nigeria. This encouraged female education in all the states of the federation. In Kaduna State, for example, enrollment of girls in schools went from 22,687 in 1968 to 182,025 in 1976 and rose to 458,158 in 1985. Nationally, the percentage of trained women teachers increased from 30 percent to about 45 percent. The number of girls in high school rose from 7.2 percent in 1975 to about 30 percent in the 1980s and to about 43.1 percent in the 1990s. In the 1970s the number of women in Nigerian universities stood at about 15 percent; in 1985 it rose to 22 percent and to 30 percent in 1990. Nationally, the number of girls enrolled in primary schools stands at 43.62 percent today (Iweriebor, 1996).

It should also be pointed out that before the introduction of the UPE serious disparities existed in the implementation of educational policies in Nigeria. For example, while pupils in the north attended elementary schools for eight years, those in the south went through the same schooling for six years. It was the UPE which streamlined the duration of schooling at the elementary level in the country. Furthermore, in 1990, primary school enrollments in Northern Nigeria stood at 5,962,659 while those in the South stood at 7,422,901. This is a ratio of 1:1.25. This ratio has remained stable since 1979 (Iweriebor, 1996). Indeed, in 1975, Bendel State (a southern state) had a female student population of 40 percent but in 1990 the population rose to 48 percent. Whereas Borno State (a northern state) which had female student enrollment of 19.3 percent in 1975 saw the figure jump to 40 percent in 1990. Girls in the north constitute 40 percent of the student population while girls in the south constitute 48 percent of the total student population (Iweriebor, 1996).

In 1944, Nigeria had 44 students per 100,000 people but today about 80 percent of the children of elementary school age are in schools. Today, there are 42 degree awarding tertiary institutions in the country with a total student enrollment of about 200,000. Of the 42 universities in Nigeria, 25 are conventional universities while 17 are specialized as follows: eight Universities of science and technology; four universities of agriculture; one mathematical center; one military academy and three language institutes devoted to the study of Nigerian languages, French and Arabic. There are seventeen federal and twenty-one state polytechnics in Nigeria. With the establishment of six technical colleges of education in the 1980s, Nigeria now has twenty federal colleges of education and thirty-six state colleges of education (Iweriebor, 1996).

From the above discussion, it could be concluded that through policy initiatives, the Nigerian government is trying to address the educational imbalance in the country so as to avert one area of potential conflict, because in this writer's opinion, the northern military leaders in Nigeria are refusing to hand over power to an elected civilian government because they are playing the educational catch-up game. Indeed, Victor Uchendu (1979a) argues that "Education is more than an instrument of national development. In post-colonial societies it is the single most important national institution that allocates present and future societal privileges..." (p. 1). He goes on to state that:

> If politics is defined as who gets what, when, and how, then access to education and distribution of the resources which facilitate this access are very political. Disputes over the expansion rates of the educational system, qualifications for entry into higher education-whether admission should be based on a quota system or not-and the location of educational facilities can be analyzed in terms of underlying conflicts of political interests. It is partly because conflicts exist between different interest groups over public policy that politics enters matters of education. Politics also gets involved because education is the key tool for the formation of a modern social structure. Future prime ministers, vice chancellors of universities, and corporation executives are not produced on peasant farms but in our schools and colleges. (Uchendu, 1979a pp. 14-15).

Uchendu argues very forcefully that, "(t)he disparity in educational opportunities between the rural areas and the urban centers, between the areas of missionary activities and those that lacked them, and between geographic and ethnic groups in any African country is great enough and, not surprisingly, poses political problems" (p. 1). He concludes that because of its unequal stratification system, formal education makes African society one of the most unequal in the world. He warns that no country in the world has ever achieved sustained economic growth without investing substantially in education for all its people because inequality in educational training has been shown to correlate directly with inequality in the distribution of earnings (Uchendu, 1979b).

END NOTES

1. The terms traditional, African and Nigerian education have been used in this work interchangeably to refer to the type of education which was carried out in Nigeria and the whole of Africa in pre-colonial times.

2. I am indebted to Okonkwo (1985) for this concept. However, I have used these illustrations for reasons, purposes and context different from that of Dr. Okonkwo. Also, see Kofi Awoonor's book *The Breast of the Earth* (New York: Anchor Press/Doubleday, 1975) for a wonderful documentation of African education through the use of literature.

3. Interview with Chief Bassey Umana Edet of Ibiaku Uruan on 20 August, 1986.

4. The development of formal or Western education between the Southern and Northern Nigeria progressed so very differently that they deserve separate treatment.

5. The Ohen is a tribute paying chief to the Oba of Benin.

6. Oba is the imperial ruler of the Benin Kingdom. Benin's influence at the peak of its glory extended as far as Dahomey and the Congo (See Jacob U. Egharevba: "The City of Benin". Kraus Reprint, 1971) p. 8.

7. The Olu is the ruler of Warri, a tributary kingdom of Benin.

8. It should be pointed out that as soon as Henry Venn died his successors were to discontinue his policy of Africanization of the church.

9. Professor E. A. Ayandele, a leading authority in the history of the Baptist Mission in Nigeria states that by Central Africa, Bowen was referring to Yorubaland (Ayandele, 1968:XV).

10. Ayandele maintains that the Emirs were not inherently opposed to Christianity.

11. Ubah's contention is corroborated by Fafunwa (1974) who maintains that:

> All the northern Emirs were political and spiritual leaders of their people and would not tolerate any local or foreign interference. It was not surprising, therefore, that the advent of Christianity in Nigeria in 1842 caused a head-on collision with Islam, especially in the north where it was firmly established (p. 100).

12. A college in this context is an equivalent of a normal school or a high school.

13. The Western Region was governed by the Action Group party whose slogan was "Freedom for All and Life More Abundant". They believed that there was life more abundant when there was education for all school-age children and general enlightenment of all literate adults (see Oyewole, 1987, p. 19).

14. The East Central State was the first state in Nigeria to formally take-over schools from missions and voluntary agencies. In this study therefore, the East Central State example will be cited since other state edicts are modeled after it. The East Central state was split into Imo and Anambra states by the federal government of Nigeria in 1976. Throughout this study, East Central State will be used to refer to the two states as constituted before 1976.

15. Henry Carr was the first African inspector of schools in Nigeria. He was first appointed to the post in 1892 by the colonial government.

16. Archbishop David Mathew was the Apostolic Delegate to British Africa who in 1951 submitted a report on the relations between Voluntary Agencies and Government in the matter of education at the request of the Advisory Committee on Education in the Colonies.

REFERENCES

Abernethy, D. B. (1969). *The political dilemma of popular education: An African case.* Stanford, CA: Stanford University Press.

Achebe, C. (1965a). *No Longer at ease.* London: Heinemann.

Achebe, C. (1965b). *Things fall apart.* London: Heinemann.

Achebe, C. (1966). *A man of the people.* London: Heinemann.

Achebe, C. (1969). *Arrow of God.* Garden City, NY: Anchor books.

Adamu, H. A. (1973). *The North and Nigerian unity: Some reflections on the political, social and educational problems of Northern Nigeria.* Lagos: The Daily Times Press.

Adaralegbe, A. (1976). The role of the federal and state governments in the UPE scheme. In N. A. Nwagwu (Ed.), *Universal primary education in Nigeria: Issues, prospects and problems* (pp. 47-62). Benin City, Nigeria: Ethiope Publishing Corporation.

Adebo and education. (1971, November). *West Africa.*

Afigbo, A. E. (1968). The background to the Southern Nigerian education code of 1903. *Journal of the Historical Society of Nigeria, 4*(2), 197-225.

Afigbo, A. E. (1978). The mission, the state and education in South-Eastern Nigeria. In E. Fashole-Luke, R. Gray, A. Hastings & G. Tasie (Eds.), *Christianity in independent Africa,* (pp. 176-192). Ibadan: Ibadan University Press.

Afigbo, A. E. (1980). Christian missions and secular authorities in South-Eastern Nigeria from colonial times. In O. U. Kalu (Ed.), *The history of Christianity in West Africa,* (pp. 187-199). Essex: Longman Group Limited.

Aguolu, C. C. (1979). The role of ethnicity in Nigerian education. *The Journal of Negro Education, 48*(4), 513-529.

Ajayi, J. F. A. (1961). Nineteenth century origins of Nigerian nationalism. *Journal of the Historical Society of Nigeria, 2*(2), 196-210.

Ajayi, J. F. A. (1965). *Christian missions in Nigeria 1841-1891: The making of a new elite*. Evanston: Northwestern University Press.

Ajayi, J. F. A. (1980). Henry Venn and the policy of development. In O. U. Kalu (Ed.), *The history of Christianity in West Africa* (pp. 63-75). Essex: Longman Group Limited.

Akpan, N. U. (1972). *The struggle for secession, 1966-1970*.London: Frank Cass.

Amadi, L. E. (1979). Public education edict, 1970; Educational transition in East Central state, Nigeria. *Journal of Negro Education, 48*(4), 530-543).

Amalaha, B. M. (1976). UPE in relation to guidance, counseling and school social work. In N. A. Nwagwu (Ed.), *Universal primary education in Nigeria: Issues, perspects and problems* (pp. 73-83). Benin City, Nigeria: Ethiope Publishing Corporation.

Asiwaju, A. I. (1972). Ashby revisited: A review of Nigeria's educational growth, 1961-1971. *African Studies Review, 15* (1), 1-15.

Awoonor, K. (1975). *The breast of the earth: A survey of the history, culture and literature of Africa south of the Sahara.* New York: Anchor Press/Doubleday.

Ayandele, E. A. (1967). *The missionary impact on modern Nigeria 1842-1914: A political and social analysis.* New York: Humanities Press.

Ayandele, E. A. (1968). Introduction. In T. J. Bowen. *Adventure and missionary labors in several countries in Africa from 1849 to 1856.* 2nd ed. London: Frank Cass.

Ayandele, E. A. (1969). Traditional rulers and missionaries in pre-colonial West Africa. *Tarikh, 3*(1), 23-37.

Ayandele, E. A. (1979). *Nigerian historical studies.* London: Frank Cass.

Ayandele, E. A. (1980). The missionary factor in Northern Nigeria 1870-1918. In O. U. Kalu (Ed.), *The history of Christianity in West Africa*, (pp. 133-158). Essex: Longman Group Limited.

Baldwin, D. E. & Baldwin, C. M. (1976). *The Yoruba of Southwest Nigeria: An indexed bibliography* (Boston: G. K. Hall & Co).

Bassey, M. O. (1989). *The politics of education in Nigeria: The case of government take-over of schools in the Cross River and Kano States.* Unpublished doctoral dissertation, Rutgers, The State University of New Jersey.

Bassey, M. O. (1991). Missionary rivalry and educational expansion in southern Nigeria, 1885-1932. *The Journal of Negro Education, 61*(1), 36-46.

Berman, E. H. (1975). *African reactions to missionary education.* New York: Teachers College Press.

Beti, M. (1965). *Mission to Kala.* London: Heinemann.

Boahen, A. A. (1966). *Topics in West African history.* London: Longman Group Limited.

Bowen, T. J. (1968). *Adventures and missionary labors in several countries in Africa from 1849 to 1856* (2nd ed.) London: Frank Cass.

Bowman, M. J. & Anderson, C. A. (1963). Concerning the role of education in development. In C. Geertz (Ed.), *Old societies and new states: The quest for modernity in Asia and Africa.* New York: Free Press.

Boyd, W. (1965). *The history of western education.* New York: Barnes and Noble.

Bray, M. (1981). *Universal primary education in Nigeria: A study of Kano state.* London: Routledge and Kegan Paul.

Burns, A. (1958). *History of Nigeria.* London: George Allen and Unwin Ltd.

Buxton, T. F. (1839). *The African slave trade and its remedy.* London: Frank Cass.

Callaway, B. (1987). *Muslim Hausa women in Nigeria: Tradition and change.* Syracuse: Syracuse University Press.

Chukunta, N. K. O. (1978). Education and national integration in Africa: A case study of Nigeria. *African Studies Review 21*(2), 67-76.

Clarke, P. B. (1978). Islam, education and the development process in Nigeria. *Comparative Education, 14*(2), 133-141.

Clarke, P. B. (1980). The methods and ideology of the Holy Ghost Fathers in Eastern Nigeria 1885-1905. In O. U. Kalu (Ed.), *The history of Christianity in West Africa,* (pp. 36-62). Essex: Longman Group Limited.

Clarke, P. B. (1982). *West Africa and Islam: A study of religious development from the 8th to the 20th century.* London: Edward Arnold.

Coleman, J. S. (1965a). Introduction: Education and political development. In J. S. Coleman (Ed.), *Education and political development,* (pp. 3-32). Princeton: Princeton University Press.

Coleman, J. S. (1965b). Introduction to part I. In J. S. Coleman (Ed.), *Education and political development,* (pp. 35-50). Princeton: Princeton University Press.

Cooke, C. M. (1978). Church, state and education: The Eastern Nigeria experience, 1950-1967. In E. Fashole-Luke, R. Gray, A. Hastings & G. Tasie (Eds.), *Christianity in independent Africa,* (pp. 193-206). Ibadan: Ibadan University Press.

Cookey-Gam, S. E. (1980). The philosophy of education during the era of inception of Western education into Nigeria 1842-1900. *Butescope, 2,* 5-9.

Crowder, M. (1962). *The story of Nigeria.* London: Faber and Faber.

Crowder, M. (1966). *A short history of Nigeria.* New York: Frederick A. Praeger, Publishers.

Crowder, M. (1968). *West Africa under colonial rule.* Evanston: Northwestern University Press.

Crowder, M. (1978). *Colonial West Africa.* London: Frank Cass.

Diejomaoh, V. P. (1972). The economics of the Nigerian conflict. In J. Okpaku (Ed.), *Nigeria: Dilemma of nationhood* (pp. 318-365). New York: The Third Press.

Dike, K. O. (1966). The teaching of Arabic in Nigeria. *Kano Studies*, No. 2. July.

Doi, A. R. (1978). Islam in Nigeria: Changes since independence. In Fashole-Luke et al (Eds.), *Christianity in independent Africa* (pp. 334-353). Ibadan: Ibadan University Press.

Education in crises. (1985, December). *West Africa.*

Egharevba, J. U. (1968). *A short history of Benin.* Ibadan: Ibadan University Press.

Egharevba, J. U. (1971). *The City of Benin.* Nendeln: Kraus Reprint.

Ekechi, F. K. (1972). *Missionary enterprise and rivalry in Igboland 1857-1914.* London: Frank Cass.

Emecheta, B. (1974). *Second-class citizens.* Glasgow: William Collins Sons.

Emecheta, B. (1978). *The bride price.* Glasgow: William Collins Sons.

Esen, A. J. A. (1976). UPE in Nigeria: Need and rationale. In N. A. Nwagwu (Ed.), *Universal primary education in Nigeria: Issues, prospects and problems* (pp. 28-34). Benin City, Nigeria: Ethiope Publishing Corporation.

Fafunwa, A. B. (1971). *A history of Nigerian higher education.* London: Macmillan.

Fafunwa, A. B. (1974). *History of education in Nigeria.* London: George Allen and Unwin.

Fajana, A. (1970). Missionary education policy in Nigeria: 1842-1882. *West African Journal of Education XIV.*

Fajana, A. (1976). A brief history of education in Nigeria. In N. A. Nwagwu (Ed.), *Universal primary education in Nigeria: Issues, prospects and problems,* (pp. 17-27). Benin City, Nigeria: Ethiope Publishing Corporation.

Fawehinmi, G. (1974). *The people's right to free education.* Lagos: John West Publications.

Federal Department of Information (n.d.). *Wheels of progress: Qualitative education.* Lagos: Government Printer.

Federal Government of Nigeria. (1977). *National policy on education.* Lagos: Government Printer.

Federal Ministry of Economic Development. (1975). *Third National Development Plan 1975-1980.* Lagos: Government Printer.

Federal Ministry of Education. (1986a). *Statistics of education in Nigeria 1980-1984.* Lagos: Government Printer.

Federal Ministry of Education. (1986b). *Statistics of education in Nigeria.* Lagos: Government Printer.

Gambari, S. (1997). *Destination Nigeria: A guide to mixing business with pleasure in Nigeria.* Tarrytown, NY: Ramat Publishing Inc.

Gbadamosi, G. O. (1967). The establishment of Western education among Muslims in Nigeria 1896-1926. *Journal of the Historical Society of Nigeria, 4*(1), 89-115.

Gesinde, S. A. (1976). The future of UPE graduates. In N. A. Nwagwu (Ed.), *Universal primary education in Nigeria: Issues, prospects and problems*, (pp. 106-114). Benin City, Nigeria: Ethiope Publishing Corporation.

Gray, R. (1980). The origins and organizations of the nineteenth century missionary movement. In O. U. Kalu (Ed.), *The history of Christianity in West Africa*, (pp. 14-21). Essex:Longman Group, Limited.

Harbison, F. & Myers, C. A. (1964). *Education, manpower, and economic growth: Strategies of human resource development.* New York: McGraw-Hill.

Hatch, J. (1970). Nigeria: *The seeds of disaster.* Chicago: Henry Regnery Company.

Ifemesia, C. C. (1980). The 'civilizing' mission of 1841: Aspects of an episode in Anglo-Nigerian relations. In O. U. Kalu (Ed.), *The history of Christianity in West Africa*, (Pp. 81-102). Essex: Longman Group Limited.

Ikejiani, O.(Ed.) (1965). *Education in Nigeria.* New York: Frederick A. Praeger.

Iweriebor, I. (1996). Nigeria: Understanding education. *West Africa*, January 15, pp. 68-69.

Izuchi, N. I. (1986). *An evaluation of the implementation of Nigeria's national policy on education at the secondary school level.* (Unpublished Ph.D. dissertation, University of Pittsburgh).

Johnson, S. (1966/1921). *The history of the Yorubas: From the earliest times to the beginning of the British protectorate.* London: Routledge & Kegan Paul Ltd.

Journals of the Rev. James Frederick Schon and Mr. Samuel Crowther: Expedition up the Niger in 1841. (1970). (2nd ed.) London: Frank Cass.

Kalu, O. U. (Ed.) (1980). *The history of Christianity in West Africa.* Essex: Longman Group Limited.

Kurian, G. T. (1988). Nigeria. In G. T. Kurian (Ed.), *World education encyclopedia.* New York: Facts on File Publications, 945-952.

Last, M. (1967). *The Sokoto caliphate.* New York: Humanities Press.

Laye, C. (1959). *The African child.* London: Fontana/Collins.

Letter from Calabar. (1971, October). *West Africa.*

Lugard, L. (1965). *The dual mandate in British tropical Africa.* (5th ed.). London: Frank Cass.

Madike, F. U. (1983). State control of education: A critical philosophical analysis. In N. Okoh (Ed.), *Professional education: A book of readings,* (pp. 52-57). Benin City, Nigeria: Ethiope Publishing Corporation.

Mbiti, J. S. (1970). *African religions and philosophy.* Garden City: Anchor Books.

McClelland, D. (1966). Does education accelerate economic growth? *Economic development and cultural change, 14*(3), 257-278.

Meek, C. K. (1969). *The Northern tribes of Nigeria.* New York: Negro Universities Press.

Moumouni, A. (1968). *Education in Africa.* London: Andre Deutsch.

Naylor, W. S. (1905). *Daybreak in the dark continent.* New York: Young Peoples Missionary Movement.

Nduka, O. (1964). *Western education and the Nigerian cultural background.* Ibadan, Nigeria: University Press Limited.

Nduka, O. (1976). Background to the foundation of Dennis Memorial Grammar School, Onitsha. *Journal of the Historical Society of Nigeria, 8*(3), 69-92.

Nigerian education: The North-South gap. (1970, July). *West Africa.*

Nigeria: Kano's education policy. (1972, February). *West Africa.*

Nigeria: What philosophy of education? (1973, January). *West Africa.*

Nigeria: Education under scrutiny. (1985, December). *West Africa.*

Nigeria: Education in doldrums. (1987, November). *West Africa.*

Nnoli, O. (1979). Education and ethnic politics in Nigeria. In V. C. Uchendu (Ed.), *Education and politics in Africa.* Buffalo, New York: Conch Magazine Limited.

Nwabara, S. N. (1977). *Iboland: A century of contact with Britain 1860-1960*. Kent: Hodder and Stoughton.

Nwagwu, N. A. (Ed.) (1976). *Universal primary education in Nigeria: Issues, prospects and problems*. Benin City, Nigeria: Ethiope Publishing Corporation.

Nwagwu, N. A. (1976). The global commitment to popular education. In N. A. Nwagwu (Ed.), *Universal primary education in Nigeria: Issues, prospects and problems* (pp. 1-16). Benin City, Nigeria: Ethiope Publishing Corporation.

Nwosu, S. N. (1976). Recruitment and training of teachers for the universal primary education. In N. A. Nwagwu (Ed.), *Universal primary education in Nigeria: Issues, prospects and problems* (pp. 63-72). Benin City, Nigeria: Ethiope Publishing Corporation.

Oduyoye, A. M. (1978). *The planting of Christianity in Yorubaland, 1842-1888*. Ibadan, Nigeria: Daystar Press.

Ogunko, G. (n.d.). Abolition of private primary schools. In *Why private primary schools must go*. Lagos State Government Publication.

Okeke, A. N. (1976). Planning effectively for UPE. In N. A. Nwagwu (Ed.), *Universal primary education in Nigeria: Issues, prospects and problems* (pp. 35-46). Benin City, Nigeria: Ethiope Publishing Corporation.

Okoh, N. (1983). State control of education in Nigeria: Another perspective. In N. Okoh (Ed.) *Professional education: A book of readings* (pp. 58-63). Benin City, Nigeria: Ethiope Publishing Corporation.

Okoh, N. (Ed.) (1983). *Professional education: A book of readings*. Benin City, Nigeria: Ethiope Publishing Corporation.

Okonkwo, C. E. (1985). Education and the African novel: Perceptions of culture in crisis. *Journal of African Studies, 12*(2), 103-110.

Oliver, R. (1967). *The missionary factor in East Africa*. London: Longman.

Oyewole, A. (1987). *Historical dictionary of Nigeria*. Metuchen: The Scarecrow Press.

Oyono, F. (1969). *The old man and the medal*. London: Heinemann.

Oyono, F. (1974). *Boy*. New York: Collier Books.

Perham, M. (1965). Introduction. In Lugard, L. *The dual mandate in British tropical Africa* (5th ed.). London: Frank Cass.

Perkins, W. A. & Stembridge, J. H. (1962). *Nigeria: A descriptive geography.* London: Oxford University Press.

Popoola, O. (n.d.). The case against private schools. In *Why private primary schools must go.* Lagos State Government Publication.

Public education edict, 1970: East Central state of Nigeria.(Gazette No. 37, January 21, 1971). Enugu: East Central State Government.

Ryder, A. F. C. (1960). Missionary activity in the Kingdom of Warri to the early nineteenth century. *Journal of the Historical Society of Nigeria, 2*(1), 1-25.

Ryder, A. F. C. (1961). The Benin Missions. *Journal of the Historical Society of Nigeria, 2*(2), 231-257.

Ryder, A. F. C. (1969). *Benin and the Europeans.* New York: Humanities Press.

Smith, R. (1969). *Kingdoms of the Yoruba.* London: Methuen & Co Ltd.

Solarin, G. L. (nd). Why private primary schools must go for good. In *Why private primary schools must go.* Lagos State Government Publication.

Solaru, T. T. (1964). *Teacher training in Nigeria.* Ibadan: Ibadan University Press.

Taiwo, C. O. (Ed.) (1969). *Henry Carr: Lectures and speeches.* Ibadan, Nigeria: Oxford University Press.

Taiwo, C. O. (1975). *Henry Carr: An African contribution to Education.* Ibadan: Oxford University Press.

Talbot, P. A. (1969). *The peoples of Southern Nigeria* (Vol 4). London: Frank Cass.

The Education crisis. (1988, September). *West Africa.*

Tibenderana, P. K. (1977). The making and unmaking of the Sultan of Sokoto, Muhammadu Tambari: 1922-1931. *Journal of the Historical Society of Nigeria, 9*, 91-134.

Tibenderana, P. K. (1983). The emirs and the spread of Western education in Northern Nigeria, 1910-1946. *Journal of African History, 24*(4), 517-534.

Tibenderana, P. K. (1985). The beginnings of girls' education in the native administration schools in Northern Nigeria, 1930-1945. *Journal of African History, 26*(1), 93-109.

Trimingham, J. S. (1962). *A history of Islam in West Africa.* Oxford: Oxford University Press.

Ubah, C. N. (1976). Problems of Christian missionaries in the Muslim emirates of Nigeria. *Journal of African Studies, 3*(3), 351-371.

Uchendu, V. C. (1979a). Introduction. In V. C. Uchendu (Ed.). *Education and politics in Africa.* Buffalo, New York: Conch Magazine Limited.

Uchendu, V. C. (1979b). Education and the public interest: The politics of the public domain. In V. C. Uchendu (Ed). *Education and politics in tropical Africa* (pp. 280-294). New York: Conch Magazine Limited.

Udo, E. A. (1980). The missionary scramble for spheres of influence in South-eastern Nigeria 1900-52. In O. U. Kalu (Ed.). *Christianity in West Africa.* (pp. 159-186). Essex: Longman Group Limited.

Webster, J. B. (1963). The Bible and the Plough. *Journal of the Historical Society of Nigeria, 2*(4), 418-434.

West Africa (1995, September 18-24). *Nigeria: Stand and Deliver.*

Whitaker, C. S. Jr. (1970). *The politics of tradition, continuity and change in Northern Nigeria 1946-1966.* Princeton: Princeton University Press.

APPENDIX A

The Nigerian 6-3-3-4
System of Education at a Glance

The 6-3-3-4 Education System at a Glance

Philosophy: The philosophy of Nigerian education is based on "the integration of the individual into a sound and effective citizen and equal educational opportunities for all citizens of the nation at the primary, secondary and tertiary levels, both inside and outside the formal school system."

Objectives: The objectives of the national policy on education are:

(a)   the inculcation of national consciousness and national unity;

(b)   the inculcation of the right type of values and attitudes for the survival of individual in the Nigerian society;

(c)   the training of the mind in the understanding of the world around, and

(d)   the acquisition of appropriate skills, abilities and competences, both mental and physical, as equipment for the individual to live in and contribute to the development of his society.

- Six years of Primary Education

- Three years of Junior Secondary School Education (JSS).

- Three years of Senior Secondary/post JSS Education.

- Higher education of varying periods provided a first degree in a university shall not be of less than 4 years duration for holders of Senior School Certificate.

The Nigerian system of education is organized in stages consisting of pre-primary, primary, secondary in two-tiers of (i) Junior and (ii) Senior, and Higher Education.

(A) Pre-Primary Education

Pre-primary education is the education given in an educational institution to children from the age of about three, prior to their entering the primary school.

(B) Primary Education

This is education given to children who must have attained the age of 6, for a period of six years.

The objectives include the preparation for a broad-based education with emphasis on the attainment of permanent and functional literacy and numeracy and effective communication skills.

Curriculum Offerings include:

(i) Language study
(ii) Integrated Science
(iii) Mathematics
(iv) Social Studies
(v) Cultural Arts
(vi) Health and Physical Education
(vii) Religious Instruction
(viii) Agriculture and
(ix) Home Economics

Evaluation and Certification: Progress and Certification are based on continuous, over-all guidance - oriented assessment by teachers and headmasters.

(C) Secondary Education

Secondary education is given in two stages: junior and senior secondary, each of three years duration (total of six years). The first stage runs classes of J.S.I., J.S. II and J.S. III while the second stage runs classes of S.S.I, S.S. II and S. S. III.

The broad aims of secondary education are preparation for useful living within the society and for higher education.

Junior Secondary School (J. S. S.) Education

The J. S. S. is both prevocational and academic. Every student offers the following subjects:

1. Mathematics
2. English
3. Language of the Environment
4. One major Nigerian Language
5. Integrated Science
6. Social Studies
7. Creative Arts (Music & Art)
8. Practical Agriculture
9. Religious Studies
10. Physical Education
11,12. Two Pre-Vocational Subjects

The pre-vocational subjects from which any two may be selected are:

1. Introductory Technology
2. Local Crafts
3. Home Economics
4. Business Studies

Schools which have the required facilities may also teach any or both of the non-vocational electives which are:

1. Arabic Studies
2. French

Evaluation and Certification are based on the continuous assessment method and an end-of-course examination conducted by the appropriate Ministry of Education leading to the award of the Junior School Certificate (J.S.C.)

At the end of the J.S.S. successful students may proceed to the second stage of secondary education. There are three types at this stage: Senior Secondary Schools, Technical Colleges and Teachers Colleges. Placement of the child in any one of these depends on his/her ability, aptitude and interest.

The curricula of Technical Colleges and Teachers' Colleges are geared towards craftsmanship and teacher training respectively. In senior secondary schools, however, all students must compulsorily offer:

1. English Language
2. One Nigerian Language
3. Mathematics

4. One of Physics, Chemistry and Biology
5. One of Literature in English, History and Geography
6. Agricultural Science or a Vocational subject

In addition to the above, every student must offer three elective subjects, not already offered as core subjects, and may drop one of these electives in the third year. The elective subjects are:

1.	Additional Mathematics	15.	Geography
2.	Agricultural Science	16.	Government
3.	Arabic Studies	17.	Health Science
4.	Auto-mechanics	18.	History
5.	Bible Knowledge	19.	Home Economics
6.	Biology	20.	Islamic Studies
7.	Book-keeping	21.	Metal Work
8.	Chemistry	22.	Music
9.	Commerce	23.	Physical Education
10.	Economics	24.	Physics
11.	Electronics	25.	Shorthand
12.	English Literature	26.	Technical Drawing
13.	Fine Art	27.	Typewriting
14.	French	28.	Woodwork

Evaluation and Certification are based on the continuous assessment method and a national examination conducted by the West African Examination Council (W.A.E.C.) leading to the award of the Senior School Certificate (S.S.C.).

(D) Higher Education

Higher education is post-secondary education given in either a University, a Polytechnic, a College of Education/Advanced Teachers' College, School of Agriculture, School of Forestry, Nursing School, etc. or a Correspondence College.

Objectives of higher education include the development of intellectual capacity to understand and appreciate the environment; and the acquisition of appropriate physical and intellectual skills necessary for the development of both the individual and his society.

Higher education is the stage of specialization. The minimum entry qualification into this stage is the Senior School Certificate (S.S.C.). Most basic courses in the university run for four years. However, professional courses may run for five or more years.

Colleges of Education/Advanced Teachers' Colleges run three year courses leading to the Nigeria Certificate in Education (N.C.E.)

Polytechnic courses are in two phases, each of two-year duration leading to the award of the National Diploma (N.D.) And Higher National Diploma (H.N.D.) respectively.

Source: Implementation Committee, National Policy on Education, Federal Ministry of Education, Lagos, Nigeria (n.d.)

INDEX

A Man of the People, 14
A Man of Worth, 14
Abacha, General Sani, 9
Abdulkadir, the emir of Ilorin, 52
Abdullah Kadiri, 53
Abeokuta, 30, 31, 34, 35, 75, 77, 78
Abeokuta Grammar School, 79
Abernethy, D.B,, xviii, 66, 80, 96, 98, 101, 103
abilities and competences, 143
ability, 145
Abo, 67, 68
Abuja, 5
Abyssinia, xviii
Abyssinia (now Ethiopia), 61
academic, 144
accident of birth, 100
accountants, 81
Achebe, 13, 14
Achebe's Things Fall Apart, 16
Achimota graduates, 116
acquisition of appropriate skills, 143
Acrobatic, 16
Acrobatic display, 13
Acting Lieutenant-Governor, 56
Acting Secretary, 74
Action Group, 132
Adamu, H.A., 107, 109
additional mathematics, 146
Adebo Commission, 117
Adefarasin, 91
Adjunct of the Church, 44
administration, 54. 114
administrators, 50
administrative experience, 89
Administrative personnel, 21
administrative positions, 81
Ado-Ekiti, 75
Adolescent, 15
Adult education, 89, 90, 91, 104
Adult literacy, 89
Adulthood, 12

Adults, 16, 89
advanced college, 71
advanced education, 73
advanced instruction 38
adversaries, 71
Advisory Committee on Education, 132
Advisory Committee on Education in the Colonies, 99
Affection, 12
Afigbo, A.E., 85, 95-97
Africa, xviii, 7, 12-14, 28-30, 36, 61, 63, 64, 91, 92, 115, 131
African, 14, 96, 116, 131
African Administration, 110
African by blood, 118
African catechists, xvii
African child, 16
African children, 12, 16
African Church, 66, 75
African Church Movement, 66
African continent, 3
African countries, 114
African culture, 97
African education, 12, 13
African Evangelical Mission, 94
African inspector of schools in Nigeria, 132
African interior, 2
African lands, 2, 3
African literature, 13
African men, xviii, 23, 24, 30, 35, 40
African middle class, xvii
African middle class elites, 29
African parent, 99
African rulers, 3
African Slave Trade and its Remedy, 29
African society, 12
African tales, 15
African teacher, 37
African topography, 16

Africanization, 30, 37, 131
Africans, 13, 97
Age group, 15
Agrarian society, 16
Agriculatural, 96
agricultural development, 40
Agricultural education, 18
Agricultural Science, 146
Agriculture, 18, 29-31. 89, 96, 114, 144
Aguiyi-Ironsi, Major General J.T.U., 111, 112
Ahmadu Bello University, 108
Ahmed, 52
aim of education, 85
Ajayi, J.F. Ade, 63
Akpakpava, 24
Aku (Yoruba), 33
Al-Azhar in Cairo, 21
alienated, 102
allocated status, 102
altar furnishings, 24
Alvarez, 73
Amadi, L.E., 119
ambassador, 24
America, 28
American Baptist missionaries, 42
American evangelist, 35
Anglican Church 28, 66
Anglican stronghold, 96
Anglicans, xviii, 61, 62
animal behavior, 16
animals, 19
Annear, 34
Annual Report for the Southern Provinces of Nigeria, 94
antagonism, 61
ante-room, 27
anti-British activities, 54
anti-Fulani, 55
anti-missionary, 83
Apostles, 70, 71
Apostolic Delegate in British Africa, 132
appreciate the environment, 146
apprenticed, 19
apprentices, 38, 85
apprenticeship, 17
aptitude, 145
Arabic, 20, 21
Arabic grammar, 2, 82,
Arabic literature, 82
Arabic studies, 48, 145, 146
Arabs, 22
arithmetic, 21, 46
arms, 23-25
army, 112
army of British magistrates, 6
Arnett, E.J., 51
Article 26 of the Declaration, 100
artisans, 87
Asaba, 3, 77
Asabia, 91
Asabia Commission, 117
ascriptive status, 102
Ashby Commission, 114
Asia, 28
Assessment on the basis of efficiency, 88
Assistant Director, 88
associations, 23
astrology, 21
Atlantic Ocean, 1
atmosphere of war, 64
attitudes, 11, 143
Atundaolus, E.A., 77
Augustinian missionaries, 26
authority, 13, 96
autobiography, 115
Auto-mechanics, 146
Awka Training College, 74
Awolowo, Chief Obafemi, 115
Awoonor, Kofi, 17
Ayandele, E.A., 54, 57, 66, 67, 77, 83, 98, 131
Azande, 19

Azikiwe, Nnamdi, 77, 115

Babamubonis, 77
Babangida, Ibrahim, 8
Badagry, 30, 33-35, 39, 62, 103
Badagry on Christmas Eve, 34
Baikie, Dr., 42
bait, 64
balancing, 16
Balewa, Alhaji Tafawa, 8
Banjo, 91
Banks of the Niger, 3
Baptism, 25, 27
Baptist Academy, 36
Baptist Boys' High School, 79
Baptist Convention of Southern
   United States of America, 35
Baptist Mission, 131
Baptist Training College, 79
Baptists, 35, 36, 75
Baptists from the (American)
   Southern Baptist Convention, 28
Baptized, 24, 70
Basden, G.T., 74
Bassa, 42
bathing, 19
Baylis, F., 55, 72, 73
beads, 23
bearing, 15
beggar, 22
beliefs, 11
Bell, H.H., 46
Bello, Sir Ahmadu, 109
Benin, 4, 23-27, 78
Benin City Government School, 38
Benin embassy, 23
Benin Kingdom, 2
Benin Republic, 1
Bennett, P.A., 68
Benue, 68
Benue river, 1
Berlin, 3
Berlin Act, 2

Berlin Conference, xix, 3, 62
Beti, Mongo, 13
Bible, 29, 31, 67, 68, 72, 103
Bible knowledge, 146
Bible stories, 43
Bibles, 34
Biblical walls of Jericho, 25
Bida, 5, 42, 43, 48, 55
Bida primary school, 53
Birnin Kebbi, 56, 57
Birnin Kebbi elementary school, 52
Birnin Kebbi middle school, 57
Bishop of Sao Thome, 27
Bismarck, Prince Otto von, 2
Black man, 68
Blacksmithing, 19, 31
blacksmiths, 38, 47
Board of Education, 88, 93
boarders, 117
body politic, 98
Bonny, 41
Bonny Government College, 71
Bonny Government School, 38
Book Keeping, 71, 146
book-learning, 68, 81
books, 24, 103, 118
Borgu, 3, 5
Bornu, 20. 42, 48, 57
Bouche, Father Pierre, 39
Bourdieu, Pierre, 102
Bowen, Thomas, 35, 36, 42, 63, 131
boys, xvii, 14, 16, 19, 31, 37, 55, 95,
   105106
brand of religion, 118
bravery, 13
bribery, 3
bricklayers, 38
Brides, 19
brig Margaret, 33
Britain, 2-4, 44, 55, 61, 62, 84, 115
Britain's greatest rival, xviii
Britain's unruly colony, xviii
British, 4-8, 35, 44, 51, 52, 54, 98

British Administration, 7, 55-57, 59, 83, 110
British administrators, 45
British assistants, 57
British authorities, 50
British authority, 55
British by culture, 118
British colonial authorities, 53
British Colonial Goverment's Official Policy, 81
British Consul-General, 86
British Control, 4, 81
British culture and control, 29
British Empire, 6
British expeditions, 55
British flag, 5, 34
British forces, 4
British Colonial Office, 4
British Colonial Secretary, 4
British Government, 3, 4, 29, 40, 86
British Government's Position, 86
British High Commissioner, 44
British Indirect Rule, 5
British Indirect Rule in Nigeria, 5
British Interest, 3
British masters, 51
British maxims, 5
British missionaries, 83
British official policy, 103
British officials, 6, 45, 54, 83
British policy, 57
British pressure, 53
British Protectorate, 3
British Protectorate of Lagos, 3
British Resident, 45
British rule, 50
British territories, 7
British West African Settlements, 93
Broghero, Rev. Father, 39
bronze work, 19
Brooke, Graham Wilmot, 42
brother, 13, 52
brotherliness, 12

Buganda,, xviii, 61
Buhari, Major General Mohammed, 8
building, 87
Bura, 1
Burdon, Major, 6, 43
burial, 19
bush, 18
Business concerns, 81
business of education, 97
Business Studies, 145
Buxton, 29, 36
buyers, 81

Calabar, 4, 36-38, 40, 63, 70, 77, 78, 86, 116
Calabar Chiefs, 36
Calabar traders, 37
Cambridge, 42
Cambridge University Mission Party, 42
Cameron, Sir Donald, 7
Cameron's efforts, 7
Cameroon, 1, 78
Campaign Against Ignorance, 89
cannon, 24
cantonment schools, 46
Capuchins, 26
car, 116
car advance, 116
care for children, 19
Carnoy, M., 102
carpenters, 30, 38, 47
carpentry, 31
Carr, Henry Rawlinson, 93, 132
Carter, Sir Gilbert, 4
carts, 48
carving, 13
Castles, 2
catechists, 31, 70, 81
Catholic Bishops, 99
Catholic child, 7, 70
Catholic faith, 27

Catholic High School, 73
Catholic institutions, 40
Catholic leadership, 71
Catholic Mission, 28, 40, 69
Catholic missionaries, xviii
Catholic Priests, 69
Catholic rivals, 75
Catholic school, 42
Catholic Superior, 64, 69
Catholic Towns, 96
Catholics, xviii, 39, 96
Caucasoid, 1
cause-and-effect, 29
Central Africa, xviii, 35, 61, 131
Central Branch, 2
Central Saharan, 2
Central School, 74, 99
certificated teachers, 116
certificates, 89
19th Century Mission, 28
Chad, 1
Chamberlain, Lord, 4
Chancellor of Germany, 2
chapel, 39
Character, 14, 15
character-building, 13
character training, 15
charitable Muslims, 22
charity, 20, 22
Charter, 3
Chartered companies, 2
Chiefs, 3, 6, 17, 24, 36, 41, 44, 58, 96
chief's sons, 43
Child, 15, 16
Children, 17, 19, 27, 67, 68, 70, 73, 75, 100, 103, 105, 106, 108, 118
Children in Nigeria, 108
Children of commoners, 59
Children's education, 99
Chisholm, Andrew, 37
chorus, 17
Christ, 33, 55

Christian, 23, 24, 32-34, 39, 50, 55, 58, 80, 103
Christian boys, 32
Christian by religion, 118
Christian churches, 44
Christian content, 50
Christian education, 45, 96, 99
Christian faith, 24
Christian government,
Christian groups, 97
Christian King, 25
Christian lines, 46
Christian mission, xvii, 40, 44, 67
Christian mission education, 97
Christian mission schools, 43, 96
Christian missionaries, 7, 27, 28, 42, 44, 81, 83, 103, 115, 118
Christian missionary bodies, 23
Christian Missionary Education, 81, 82
Christian religion, 55
Christian school, 54, 83, 118
Christian teachings, 54
Christian village, 64
Christian village phase, 69
Christian-run primary schools, 81
Christianity, xviii, 23, 25-27, 29, 34, 36, 41, 45, 52, 53, 58, 63, 64, 67, 69, 76, 77, 84, 103, 104, 131
Christians, 26-28, 82, 83, 118
Church, 23, 27, 29, 34, 35, 75, 80-83, 96, 131
Church and Missionary rivalries, 81
Church and State, 67
Church Missionary Society, (CMS), 28, 29, 30, 42, 64, 67, 75, 96
Church Missionary Society Grammar School, 75
Church of England, 28
Church of Scotland, 38
Church of Scotland Mission, 116
Church rivalry, xvii, 81
Church vestments, 24

Churchmen, 75
circumcise, 27
citizens, 98
City of Benin, 131
civil services, 47
civil uprisings, 45
Civil war, 8, 92, 117
civilization, 29, 36
clan, 12
Clapham Sect, 28
classical learning, 47
cleavages along religious lines, 118
clerical, 21
clerical work, 40
clerks, 38, 46, 47, 81, 87
Clifford, Sir Hugh, 48, 49
climbing, 16
clothes, 23
CMS, 29-31, 34, 42-44, 55, 58, 62, 63, 68, 73, 80, 86, 96
CMS at Ondo and Ekiti, 75
CMS Bishop, 74
CMS Committee, 30
CMS girls, 32
CMS Grammar School, 31, 77
CMS High School, 74
CMS London Secretary, 72
CMS Mission Secretary, 68, 72
CMS missionaries, 30, 31, 35, 73
CMS missionary field, 72
CMS party, 30
CMS school curriculum, 72
CMS secondary school, 72
CMS secretary, 43, 45
Code, 88
co-education, 56
co-educational schools, 56
Coercion, 3
Coker, J.K., 66
College, 71, 132
College of Education/Advanced Teachers' College, 146, 147
Colonial administrators, 45, 98

Colonial education, 102
Colonial forces, 98
Colonial Goverment, 86, 93-95, 97, 103
Colonial Government Report, 82
Colonial regime, 97
Colonial situation, 52, 58
Colonies, 132
colonialism, 21, 97
colonialization, 102
colonize, 102
colonized individual, 102
colonizer, 102
Colony, 39, 88, 93
combat sectionalism, 92
comfort, 94
Columbin, Father, 26
Commander of the British Forces, 5
commerce, 29, 146
commercial undertaking, 98
Commission, 114, 117
Commission on Post-School Certificate and Higher Education in Nigeria, 114
Commission Report, 114
commissions, 98
commoners, 53
communal/social national needs, 101
community, 12, 88, 95
concentration, 18
Conditions of Service, 115, 117, 118
conference, 96, 106
conference of Chiefs, 53
conflict, xx
Congo, 25, 36, 39, 115, 131
Congregation, 71
Constitution, 6
Consul General, 4
consumer good, 113
consumption good, 115
continuous assessment, 145, 146
continuous over-all guidance, 144
convent school, 40

converts, 69, 93
cooking, 13
cooperative, 12
Correspondence College, 146
corrupt Emirs, 45
corruption, 89
counselor, 7
counter coup, 112
counter-culture, 82
counter-Islam, 82
country, 96, 127
coup, 8
courage, 13, 15
crafts, 19
craft center, 48
craft school, 47
craftsmanship, 145
Creative Arts (Music & Art), 145
creed, 6, 119
Creek Town, 38, 116
creeping crops, 18
crop, 16
crop fields, 30
cross, 42
Cross River group, 2
Crowther, Bishop Samuel Ajayi, 39, 63, 68, 69
cult leaders, 17
cultivation, 16
cultural, 82
Cultural Arts, 144
cultural heritage, 20, 101
cultural patterns, 11
cultures of silence, 101
cultures, 11
curiosity, 16
curriculum, 20, 50, 57, 72, 73, 86, 124, 144
curriculum of secondary education, 124
customs, 1, 11, 15, 82
cutlass, 18

d'Aveiro, John Affonso, 23
Dahomey, 39, 131
dancing, 13
dangers, 20
day schools, 31
Dayspring, 42
de Barros, 25
de Bressilac, Father, 39
de Graft, William, 34, 35, 62
deep-rooted crops, 18
defensor fidei, 59
Decree Number 34, 111, 112
Delta (Jaja of Opobo), 4
Delta city-states, 37
Delta coasts, 3
democratic principles, 102
demonstration, 13
Dennis, Archdeacon, 72, 73
Dennis Memorial Grammar School, 72, 74, 79, 80, 116
denomination, 64, 75, 80
denominational rivalries, 96
despair, 102
development, 120
development of intellectual, 146
development projects, 120
dialects, 1
Diary, 62
dictatorship, 115
Dictionary of the Yorba language, 36
Diejomaoh, V.P., 108, 112
differential impact of colonial rule, 122
differential in per capita income, 108
diffusion of educational demand, 122
dignity of labor, 124
Dike, 91
Diocesan Synod, 55, 93
Diplomatic relations, 23
Direct Apostolate, 75
Director, 56
Director and the Deputy Director of Education, 88

Director of Education, 46, 56, 88
discipline, 15, 18, 19, 87, 94
discrete, 102
disease, 102
dishonour, 14
disloyalty to the cause of a united Nigeria, 92
disparities, 127
dispensaries, 40
District, 38
District of the Northern Provinces, 54
divination, 21
divine Kinship, 25
divine revelation, 6
divine rule of kingship, 25
diviners, 17, 19
divisional school boards, 119
divorce, 13
doctors, 19
Doi, A.R.I., 82
dominant ethnic group, 102
dominant ethnic group to colonize others, 102
dominate, 112
domination, 102, 112
Domingos, Antonio Dom, 26, 27
donations, 20
doubtful character, 85
Dove, Rev. Thomas, 33, 34
downtrodden poor population, 59
drift by teachers, 118
drills, 21
drumming, 13
Dual Mandate, 94
Duke Town Primary School, 63
Duke Town Secondary School, 79
dumbfoundment, 63
Du Plessis, Professor, 98
duplication of schools, 96
dwellings, 19
dying, 19
Dual Mandate, 7

East, 32, 36, 39, 76, 90, 91, 113
East Africa, xviii, 61
East Central State, 92, 132
East Central State Education Edict, 92, 113
East of the Niger, 69
Easter, 32
Eastern governments, 109
Eastern Nigeria, xvii, 2, 62, 69-71, 76, 98, 118
Eastern region, 1, 8
Eastern regional elections, 118
Eastern states, 92
Eastern Yoruba Country, 77
Easterners 8
economic, 23, 95, 115, 120
economic consequences, 113
economic domination, 112
economic growth, 115
economic management, 101
economic progress, 115
Economics, 146
Economy, 18, 98
Edet, Bassey Umana, 131
Edgerley, Samuel, 37, 38
Edo, 1
Edos, 2, 112
educate, 53
Educated Africans, 45
Educated Native, 45
Educated Nigerians, 98, 113
Education, 11-13, 15, 27, 35, 36, 40, 46, 52-54, 59, 63, 64, 66, 69-71, 73, 76, 77, 83-87, 89, 91-97, 100, 102, 103, 105, 113, 115, 117, 119, 120, 122, 124, 126, 128, 129, 132
Education as a Fundamental Human Right, 100
Education as a Means of Political Socialization, 101
Education as an investment, 113
Education Code of 1903, 87
Education Code of 1926, 87

Education decision-making, 101
Education differential, 111, 113
Education expenditure, 89
Education Department, 39
Education laws and ordinances, 91
Education of Africans, 29
Education Ordinance, 87
Education Ordinance of 1916, 54
Education policies, 127
Education rules, 38
Education scholars, 21
Education statistics, 105
Education system, 125
Education system at a Glance, 143
Educational, 125
Educational activity, 125
Educational and national needs, 92
Educational assessment, 125
Educational attainment, 112, 113
Educational catch-up game, 128
Educational development, 48, 104
Educational disparity, 108
Educational Expansion in Nigeria, 61
Educational facilities, 128
Educational imbalance, xx, 101, 103-105, 107, 108, 121, 122, 128
Educational institution, 143
Educational matters, 88
Educational opportunities, xix, 120, 122, 128
Educational plans, 107
Educational policy, 95, 125
Educational process, 125
Educational projects, 51
Educational regions, 107
Educational revolution, 124
Educational system, 98
Educational work, 61, 84
Educationally advanced zones, 107
Educational backward areas, 108
Educational under-developed areas, 107

efficiency, 118
efficient staff, 87
efficient system of education, 93
effective communication skills, 144
effective occupation, 3
Efik, 1, 2, 40
Efiks, 112
Egbas, 40
Egypt, 46, 50, 54
Eke, Chief Abdul, 106
Ekechi, Felix, xviii, 41, 68, 73
Ekiti-Ondo, xvii, 40, 103
Eko Boys' High School, 79
electricians, 109
electronics, 146
elementary, 100
Elementary Algebra, 73
Elementary education, 100
Elementary level, 127
Elementary pupils, 120
Elementary school age, 127
Elementary schools, 38, 120, 126, 127
Elephants, 19
elites, 30
Emecheta, Buchi,, 13
Emekuku, 96
emigrants, 33
Emir, 42, 52, 57, 58
Emir of Argungu, 53, 56
Emir of Gwandu, 52
Emir of Ilorin, 3, 53, 56
Emir of Kontagora, 5
Emir of Zaria, 53, 56, 58
Emir Aliyu 'the Great', 58
emirate, 57
emirate (or imamate), 59
emirates, 51
Emirs, 6, 7, 44, 50, 51, 53, 54, 56, 59, 83
Emirs' fears, 56
Emirs of Adamawa, 53
Emirs of Argungu, 56

Emirs of Bornu, 56
Emirs of Kano, 56
Emirs of Katsina, 53, 56
Emirs of Nupe, 3, 42
Emirs of Sokoto, 5
Emir's court, 58
Emir's explanation, 57
Emir's sons, 53
emotional, 124
Empire, 2, 3
employment, 2, 122
end-of-course examination, 145
endurance, 13, 15
engineering, 77
engineering and law, 114
engineers, 38
England, xviii, 27, 61
English, 36, 37, 43, 48, 57, 67, 68, 72, 75, 81, 145
English Bible, 68
English Education, 72
English Language, 41, 43, 57, 72, 73, 145
English literature, 146
English printer, 37
English trader, 36, 37
Enlightenment, 132
enrolled, 120
equal access by, 100
equal educational opportunities, 145
equal staffing, 119
equality, 102
equalization, 123
equalizing acess, 122
equipment, 87, 199
equitable distribution, 122
equitable distribution of educational facilities, 123
esteem, 101
ethnic group, 1, 17
ethnic tensions, 8
ethical, 82
ethical behavior, 15

ethics, 82
ethnic conflicts and tensions, 123
ethnic groups and languages, 125
ethnicity, 119
European, xix, 2, 13, 17, 67, 81
European Companies, 2
European Countries, 2
European culture, 81
European Education, 81
European Evangelical Movement, 28, 56
European Language, 37
European Missionaries, xvii, xix
European Nation, 3
European Powers, 3
European rule, 98
European Technological Achievement, 67, 80
European-trained Nigerians, 81
European Women Teachers, 56
Europeans 23, 30, 31, 82, 83, 94, 116
Evaluation and Certification, 144-146
Evangelical movements, 28
Evangelistic, 85
Evangelistic objective, 84
Evangelization, 64, 69-71, 75, 103
evil and paganism, 83
ex-slaves, 30, 32
examination results, 88
examinations, 53
excellence, 94
Executive Committee, 74
existing order, 102
experimental farm, 40
experts, 98
exploitation, 102
export levels, 108
eyes, 18

facilities, 96
facilities for education, 122
Fafunwa, A. Babs, 12, 14, 22, 58, 83

false faith, 55
false prophet, 42
family, 12, 18
farming, 17, 18
farms, 31, 43
Fawehinmi, Gani, 115
Federal colleges of education, 128
Federal Commissioner for Education, 106
Federal corporations, 109
Federal establishments, 109
Federal Government, 122
Federal Government appointments, 108
Federal Government jobs, 108
Federal Government of Nigeria, 117, 123
Federal Minister of Education, 107
Federal Public Service, 106, 109, 111
Federal Services, 109
Federally controlled universities, 107
fees, 119
female education, 127
Female Institute, 31
female students, 56, 127
female teachers, 116
Fergusson, James, 33
fertile lands, 16
fetish practices, 39
feudal autocracy, 115
Few linguistic groupings, 1
Fez, 21
Fika, 57
financial constraints, 89
financial position, 100
Fine Art, 146
firearms, 23, 25
First Class Chiefs, 52
First National Development Plan, 122
First Prime Minister, 8
fish migratorial patterns, 18

fishing, 13, 16-18
fishing boats, 18
fishing grounds, 18
fishing season, 16
flexible choice, 125
folk-tales, 16
folklores, 15, 17
food, 19, 22
forbearers of Western Education, 83
forefathers, 94
foreign interference, 131
Foreign Languages, 73
foreign natives, 87
foreigner, 99, 101
formal, 19
formal education, 52, 101, 113, 124, 129
formal school system, 143
Fort Elmina, 23
Fourah Bay College, 76
fragile administration, 93
France, xviii, 2, 28, 61, 115
Franciscan Sisters, 40
free and democratic society, 122, 123
free, just and democratic society, 123
free market forces, 101
free meal, 53
Freeman, 34
Freetown, 32, 33
Freire, Paulo, 101
Freire's anxieties, 102
French, 4, 58, 98, 128, 145, 146
French Catholic missionary, 61
French Catholic missionary order, xviii
Frenchmen, 58
friends, 14, 17, 18
Fulani, 1, 5
Fulani administration, 5
Fulani impostors, 55
fulfillment, 125
functional education, 39
functional literacy, 144

functionalism, 12
fundamental change, 124
fundamental human right, 100
furniture, 49

Gallas, xviii, 61
Gambia, 87
games, 16, 17
Gbebe, 41
genealogy, 16
general efficiency of a school, 87
general progress, 87
General elections, 8
General Secretary, 46, 48
generation, 11
geographic and ethnic groups, 129
Geography, 46, 48, 146
Geometry, 73
George, 37
Germany, 2
Ghana, 2, 32
girl, 14, 19, 31, 40, 56, 57, 103, 106, 127
girls enrolled in primary schools, 127
girls in high school, 127
girls in secondary schools, 105
girls' school, 31, 56, 127
Girouard, Percy, 6, 44-46
God, 33, 34, 37, 44, 63, 70, 71
God-fearing, 32
Gold Coast, 32, 34, 87
Gold Coast (now Ghana), 46, 99
Gollmer, Rev., 30, 32
Golti, Cardinal, 63
Good Anglicans, 118
Good Baptists, 118
Good Catholics, 118
Good education, 41, 64
Good Methodists, 118
Good Muslims, 21, 118
Good Nigerians, 118
good citizen in Nigeria, 118
good weather, 18

Gordon College, 46
Gordon, the first British Inspector of Education for Southern Nigeria, 84
Gospel, 30, 34, 35, 54, 103
Government, 6, 29, 38, 44, 47, 49, 52, 56, 85, 87, 91, 93-95, 98, 109, 110, 117, 119, 126, 132, 146
Government abolished primary school fees, 120
Government College, 79
Government control of schools, 84
Government examinations, 85
Government expenditures, 108
Government grant, 117
Government intervention, 101
Government of the land, 51
Government offices, 40
Government owned and operated schools, 115
Government primary school, 116
Government reports, 74
Government schools, 48, 50, 116, 117
Government take-over, 99
Government take-over of schools, xix, 91, 100, 101, 113
Governmental system, 128
Governor, 46, 51
Governor-General of Nigeria, 58, 94
Governor-General of Nigeria's intervention, 58
Governor of Benin River, 4
Governor-General, 5, 7
Governor-General of Nigeria, 7
Gowon, General, Yakubu, 8, 107, 108, 112
grace, 25
grades A,B,C, or D, 88
graduate teacher, 116
graduates of universities, 114
grammar, 27, 36
grammar school, 40, 74, 80
Grants, 88, 95, 97

Grants Code, 1916
Grants-in-aid, 87, 94, 95, 97
great and dynamic economy, 122, 123
greater variation in the geographical spread of agencies, 122
Greek, 72
Gross National Product, 101
guidelines, 95
Gulf of Guinea, 1
guns, 25
Gwandu, 5, 48
Gwatto, 23

habits, 18
Hadith, 21
Hamitic language, 2
handmaids, 103
harbingers of Western or formal education, 27
hardship, 14
Hassan, 56
Hausa, 2, 42, 46, 48, 55, 113, 126
Hausa Association, 55
Hausa cities, 55
Hausa language, 43. 55
Hausa peasantry, 54
Hausa states, 2, 55
Hausa studies, 48
Hausa-Fulani, 1
Hausaland, 55, 83
hazardous journeys, 52
head-on collision, 84, 131
Headquarters, 62
health, 84, 122, 124
Health and Physical Education, 144
Health Science, 146
healthy growth, 20
Her Majesty's Government, 85
herbalists, 17
herbs, 19
High Commissioner, 5
High School, 73, 74, 87, 132

High School fees, 122
Higher education, 114, 126, 128, 143, 144, 146
Higher National Diploma, 147
Higher standards, 87
Hinderer, 31
hinterlands, 3, 74
History, 13, 16, 46, 48, 146
Hodder, B.W., 30
Holy Ghost Fathers, 39, 62, 64, 69, 80
home, 17
Home Economics, 144-146
homemaking, 19
honest, 12
honesty, 15
Hong Kong, 45
honour, 14, 15
Hope Waddell Training Institution, 38, 71, 79, 86
horizontal, 105
horseback, 52
house rats, 19
housewives, 19
human beings, 29
human capital, 113
human resources, 120
Human right, 100
hunger, 102
hunting season, 16, 17
husband, 13
Hussey, Mr., 56
hymns, 118

Ibadan, 4, 31, 35, 75, 77, 91, 109
Ibadan Grammar School, 79
Ibadan officers, 111
Ibi, 3, 42
Ibiaku Uruan, 131
Ibibio, 1, 2, 69
Ibo, 1, 68, 126
Ibo Boys' Institute, 79
Ibo man, 68

Ibos, 2, 8, 68, 112, 113
Ibuno, 1
Idah, 41
ideals, 20
ideas, 20
Idoma, 1
Idumwerie, 24
Ife, 2
Igala, 1
Igbariam, 70
Igbo, 67, 69, 77
Igbo Language, 67
Igbo Parentage, 67
Igbo Village, 68
Igboho, 35
Igboland, 66, 96
Igboman, 66
Igbos, 68, 76, 77
Ijala, 17
Ijaw, 1
Ijaye, 35, 40
Ijebu Terrigory, 75
Ijebu-Ode, 75
Ijebu-Ode Grammar School, 79
Ijebuland, 77
Ijesha, 40
Ijo, 2
Ikaibo, 1
Ikoku, 91
illegalities, 84
Ilmi, 21
Ilorin, 5, 42, 55, 57
imbalance, 113
imitation, 13, 16
Imoke, Dr. S.E., 98
imperialism, 98, 102
importance of language, 125
important instrument, 124
impossibility of being, 102
incantations, 16, 17
inclinations, 16
independence, 99-101
India, 54

indigenous society, 95
indirect coercion, 102
Indirect rule, 5-7, 50, 51, 55, 57
individuals, 101, 123-125, 146
Industrial Department, 38
Industrial education, 31, 40
Industrial program, 30
Industrial training, 38
Industrial work, 86
Industries, 109, 114
Industry, 29
inequalities, 122
inequality in educational training, 129
inequality in distribution of earnings, 129
inequity, 122
infamous, 38
infertile lands, 16, 18
informal training, 19
Inspector of Education, 84, 93
Inspectorate Division, 95
institutions, 13
instruments, 93
instrument of national development, 129
instrument par excellence, 123
Integrated Science, 144, 145
integrity, 15
intellectual gift, 16
intellectual level, 15
intellectual skills, 16
intellectual standpoint, 71
intellectual training, 13, 16, 17
intellectuals, 36
Intense rivalry, xviii
interdenominational rivalries, 75
interest, 145
intermediate, 87
internship, 19
interpreter, 30, 95
Introductory Technology, 145
intuition, 16

investment, 115
Investment in Education, 114
Ireland, xviii, 61
Irish brothers, 39
Islam, 20, 22, 44, 45, 82, 84, 131
Islamic education, xix, 20, 22, 45, 49, 82
Islamic history, 21
Islamic law, 21, 82
Islamic scholars, 21, 82
Islamic scholarship, 41
Islamic schools, 82
Islamic secondary schools (ilm), 82
Islamic social and religious pattern, 82
Islamic studies. 22, 48, 146
Islamic teachers, 22
Islamic Universities, 21
Italian, 25, 39
Italy, 2
Itsekiri, 26
Ivory, 23

Japan, 115
Jamaica, 38
Ja'afaru, the Emir of Zaria, 52
Jebba, 3. 42
Jehovah, 33
Jekri, 1
Jesuit, xviii, 36, 61
jihad, 45, 84
job orientation, 13
Jonas, Simon, 67, 68
Jorge, Dom, 24
judges, 50
judgment, 16
judicial, 21
judicial matters, 51
juju, 14
jumping, 16
Junior, 143
Junior and Senior Secondary, 144
Junior Secondary School, 124

Junior School Certificate, 145
Junior Secondary School Education, 143
Just and egalitarian society, 122, 123

Kabba, 5
Kaduna, 56, 83
Kaduna College, 52
Kaduna State, 127
Kaiyama, 86
Kalabari, 2
Kanawa, 58
Kanem-Bornu empire, 2
Kano, 5, 20, 43, 46, 48, 52, 56-58, 103, 105
Kano Muslim trader, 83
Kano Poet, 83
Kano school, 48
Kano State, 105, 106
Kano trader, 83
Kanuri, 1
Kanuri descent, 42
Kanuri of Northeast Nigeria, 2
Katsina, 20, 42, 43, 48, 56, 57
Katsina College, 49, 53
Katsina Teacher's Training College, 49
Kebbi, 48
Keffi, 5
key to a modernization process, 123
Khartoum, 46
killings, 112
kind, 32
King, 23, 26, 27, 36
King Eyo, 37
King Manuel, 24
King Manuwa, 40
King of Benin, 4
King or Portugal, 24
Kingdom of Shoa, xviii
Kingdoms, 2
King's College, 79
kinsman, 13

Kipo Hill, 42
knitting, 13
knowledge, 11, 102
knowledgeable, 99
Konden Diara, 14
Kontagora, 5, 42
Krapf, Johann, xviii, 61
Kurumi, 40
Kru-speaking, 2
Kuti, Rev. Ransome, 77
Kwa, 2
Kwara State, 105

laborers, 30
Lagoon, 30
Lagos, 3, 4, 23, 31, 32, 36, 39, 40, 46, 54-56, 70, 75-77, 87, 93, 109
Lagos Colony, 78
Lagos and Protectorate, 5
Lagos Grammar School, 32
Lagos State, 105, 106
Lagos Training Institution, 31
Laissez-Faire Educational Policy, 84
Lamido of Adamawa, 52
land, 12
land full of opportunities for all citizens, 123
land of bright and full of opportunities, 122
language, 1, 2
language institutes, 128
Language of the Environment, 143
Language study, 144
last days, 83
Latin, 72
Latin grammar, 27
Laws, 38, 82
Laye, Camara, 14
Leach, A.F., 27
leapfrogging operations, xviii, 62
leather workers, 47
Legal cases, 83
legitimate commerce, 29

Lejeune, Father Leon, 64, 69
Lena, Father, 70
length of primary and secondary school programs, 91
lepers, 38
LeRoy, Msgr., 64
less developed ethnic groups, 123
Lethem, 56
Liberal Arts, 114
lies, 83
Lieutenant-Governor, 7, 51
Lieutenants, 58
Life and times of Prophet Muhammad, 21
Lifelong education, 125
limited supply, 122
lingua franca, 125
literacy, 127
Literary, 93
Literary class, 82
Literary curriculum, 96
Literary education, 94
literate adults, 132
literate women, 127
Literature, 21
Literature in English, 146
Livingstonia, 38
local, 131
local administration, 53
local crafts, 145
local geography, 15
local native courts, 95
local secretary, 73
local secretary at Onitsha, 73
Lokoja, 1, 3, 5, 43
logic, 21
London, 33, 73
London Office, 73
London University Degree, 116
Lord, 41, 63, 115
love, 12
Lower Niger, 69
loyalty, 12

Lugard, 3-5
Lugard, Lord 5, 7, 42, 44-46, 94
Lugard's control, 5
Lugard's immediate successor, 44
Lugard's forces, 5
Lugard's pledge, 104
Lugard's successor, 6
Lower Benue, 5
Lutheran missionary, xviii
Lutherans, xviii, 61
Lutz, Father, 69
Lyons, 40

Macaulay, Rev. T.B., 32
Macaulay, Zachary, 28
Macdonald, Sir Claude, 4
Macedonian, 67
Mackay, A.M., xviii
Macpherson Constitution, 88, 91, 93
Maguzawa, 54
Mahdist uprising, 83
Madike, F.U., 101, 102
Makarantar Allo, 21
Makarantar Ilmi, 21
make cloth, 19
male, 116
male child, 16
malaria, 30
Mallamai, 82, 83
Mallams, 43, 46, 47, 50
Mallam's school, 46, 47
man, 14, 29
management of schools, 100
managers, 88
manners, 15
manual, 96
manual activity, 13, 17
manual work, 81
massacre, 8
markets, 84
marriage, 104
Marsh, William, 30, 31
Marshall, Sir James, 39

massacres, 112
masses, 101
master-craftsmen, 17
material world, 66
mathematical center, 128
mathematical skills, 16
mathematics, 17, 72, 144, 145
Mathew, Archbishop David, 99, 132
matrimony, 27
Mbiti, J.S., 19
McCormack, John, 30
meagre resources, 93
mechanics, 109
medical and educational services, 28
medical services, 40
medicinal herbs, 17
medicine, 21, 114
medicine men, 19
medicines, 19
memorandum, 70, 72
memorandum on higher education, 71
men, 102
Mennonite Brethren, 42
mental deficiencies, 102
merchants, xix, 36, 62
Metal Work, 146
method and practice, 11
messengers, 38
Methodism, 75
Methodist, 75
Methodist at Ijebu-Remo, 75
Methodist Boys' High School, 77, 79
Methodist Boys' High School in Lagos, 34
Methodist Church, 33
Methodist Girls' High School, 34, 79
Methodist Minister, 33
middle school, 57
Midwest, 8
milestone, 48
military, 25
Military Academy, 128

military coup, 8, 111
Military Courts, 112
Military Government, 112
Military Prefects, 112
Miller, Edward, 37, 43, 55, 58
Miller's compound, 58
millions, 114
Minister of Education, 98
minority upper class, 102
Ministry of Education, 145
misconduct, 15
Mission, 54, 85, 88, 95, 103
Mission control of schools, 85
Mission education, 95, 96
Mission headquarters, 73
Mission house, 30
Mission inspectors, 74, 88
Mission reports, 85
Mission run schools, 117
Mission Schools, 64, 80, 85, 87, 99, 116, 118, 119
Mission Secretary, 85
Mission-operated Schools, 77
Mission station, 30
Missionaries, xvii, xix, 23-25, 27, 29, 30, 34, 36, 37, 41, 45, 54, 55, 58, 59, 62, 67, 85, 93, 97, 98, 103, 113, 118
Missionary, xvii, 28, 33, 36, 62, 67, 85
Missionary bodies, 85
Missionary education, 40, 102
Missionary enterprise, 54, 98
Missionary field, 69
Missionary groups, 28
Missionary rivalry, xix, 61, 64, 69, 72, 75, 76, 80
Missionary rivalry in Nigeria, xix
Missionary societies, 29, 35, 93
Missions, 28, 67, 84-86, 92, 94, 95, 97, 98, 99, 103, 115, 118
modern educational techniques, 125
Modern Nigeria, 4, 5

modern state, 101
modern technological age, 22
modernizing influences, 50
Mohammed, General Murtala, 8
Mohammedan priests, 46
Mohammedans, 46
money, 87, 96
monogamy, 39
Monrovia Africans' Luminary, 32
moon, 18
Moor, Sir Ralph, 86
moral, 124
moral behavior, 15
moral ethos, 82
moral instruction, 87
moral qualities, 15
moral tone, 124
moral training, 15
Moslem, 55
Moslem school, 99
Moslems, 118
Mosque, 44
mother tongue, 72
mothers, 19
motor parts, 48
Moumouni, Abdou, 12, 15
Muallim, 22
Muhammad Bayero, 56
Muhammad Dikko, 56
Muhammad Ndayako, the Emir of Bida, 52
Muhammadan men, 49
Muhammadans, 48, 49
Murray, Dr. A.V., 45
Music, 146
Muslim, 20, 42, 45, 75
Muslim areas, 104
Muslim authorities, 54
Muslim Chiefs, 55
Muslim city, 42
Muslim countries, 50
Muslim education, 104
Muslim Emirates, 49, 54

Muslim Emirs, 46
Muslim intelligentsia, 59
Muslim law, 59. 83
Muslim lines, 46
Muslim North, 50
Muslim rulers, 59
Muslim schools, 118
Muslims to Christianity, 118
Muslim teachers, 21, 47, 83
Muslims, 45, 50, 54, 58, 82, 83,
mystery of reading, 68
mysticism, 82

Nana, 4
Nantes, 26
narrative learning, 102
narrow the gap, 123
Nassarawa Central Schools, 46, 47, 50
Nation, 114
Nation-building, 119
Nation state, 98
National concern, 93, 101
National consciousness, 123, 143
National Council on Education, 106
National Curriculum Conference, 91
National Development, 119, 123
National Development Plan, 122, 124
National Diploma, 147
National examination, 146
National Institution, 128
National integration, 119
National literacy rate, 126
National literate population, 127
National policy, 123-125
National Policy on Education, 120-125, 143
National unity, 123, 143
Nationalist Governments, 88, 96
nationality factors, xviii, 61
nationalize, 101, 102
nationwide strike, 116

Native Administration girls' schools, 57
Native Administration officials, 53
Native Administration schools, 52
Native Administration workers, 53
Native authorities, 7, 116
Native Authority Administration, 82
Native Chief, 7
Native Church, 74
Native Doctors, 17
Native laws, 15
Native rulers, 6
Natives, 86, 94
natural law, 6
navigational isntruments, 18
Negroid, 2
neighbours, 25
new constitution, 8
new markets, 29
New Nigerian, 112
New Testament, 43
Nduka, Otonti, 74, 80
Niger, 1, 4, 29, 39, 42, 55, 57, 68, 75
Niger Coast, 85
Niger Coast Protectorate, 4
Niger Company, 3
Niger Expedition, 30, 35, 67
Niger District, 3
Niger-Congo, 2
Niger-Congo group of languages, 2
Niger Mission, 74, 80
Nigeria, xvii-xix, 1-4, 8, 9, 11, 17, 20-23, 27, 28, 35, 36, 39, 40, 44, 49, 50, 56, 61-63, 68-70, 72, 73, 80, 83-86, 88, 91-93, 95-103, 105, 107, 108, 111-114, 117, 120-128, 131, 132
Nigeria Certificate in Education, 147
Nigeria Head of State, 107
Nigerian, 43, 100, 113, 115, 131
Nigerian Catholic Bishops, 99
Nigerian child, 17
Nigerian Civil War, 92, 108

Nigerian civilian Prime Minister, 8
Nigerian coast, 24
Nigerian crisis, 112
Nigerian economy, 113
Nigerian education, 119, 123, 124
Nigerian educated elites, 93
Nigerian education, xix
Nigerian Education Research Council, 91
Nigerian educational system, xix, 84, 117
Nigerian elites, 115
Nigerian Federation, 113
Nigerian government, xx
Nigerian Judges, 100
Nigerian Missionary field, 29
Nigerian Nation, 118
Nigerian parents, 14
Nigerian people, 114
Nigerian political scene, 77
Nigerian politician, 115
Nigerian populace, xvii
Nigerian primary schools, 126
Nigerian schools, 91, 126
Nigerian secondary schools, 126
Nigerian societies, xix, 41, 143
Nigerian teachers, 116
Nigerian Union of Teachers, 116
Nigerian Universities, 109
Nigerian workers, 117
Nigerians, xix, 1, 62, 81, 94, 96, 100, 102, 114
Nigeria's hinterland, 3
Nigeria's needs, 113
Nikki, 3
Nile, 115
Nkwerre, 96
No Longer at Ease, 13
non-formal institutions, 11
non-government grant-aided schools, 117
non-Muslim areas, 81, 103
non-Muslim northerner, 8

non-Nigerians, 99
normal school, 132
North, 1, 41, 42, 44, 45, 47, 50, 55, 57-59, 75, 81, 84, 90, 91, 103, 104, 106-109, 111, 112, 116, 120, 121, 126, 127
North and South of Nigeria, 5
North-Central, 106
North East State, 120
North-Western, 106
North-Western State, 105
Northeast, 1
Northern, 112
Northern Emirs, 57, 131
Northern military leaders, 128
Northern Missionary field, 42
Northern Nigeria, 2, 5-8, 20, 21, 41, 43-46, 48, 50, 51, 52, 54, 55, 57, 59, 81-83, 103, 104, 120, 126, 127
Northern Nigerian society, 50, 83
Northern Officers, 8, 112
Northern parts of Nigeria, 32
Northern Provinces, 46, 56
Northern Region, 8, 89, 107
Northern Region Government Service, 109
Northern Rhodesia (now Zimbabwe), 99
Northern States, 45, 105, 106
Northern States of Benue and Plateau, 105
Northerners, 45, 82, 105, 106, 107, 108, 109, 111, 112
Northwest, 1
Nsukka, 109
numbers of schools, 62
numeracy, 144
Nupe, 1, 2, 5, 43
Nupe languages, 42, 43
Nursery of the Infant Church, 54, 62
Nursing School, 146
Nwoye, 15

Oba, 4, 23, 26, 34, 35
Oba of Benin, 24, 131
Oba of Benin's Quest, 25
Oba Ovonramwen, 4
Oba's Palace, 25
Obasanjo, Lt-General Olusegun, 8
obedient, 32
Obi, 68
Obi of Onitsha, 69
objective, 99, 143
objectives of higher education, 146
Obosi, 68
observation, 16
officials, 98
Ogbelaka, 24
Ogbomosho, 75
Ogoja, 69, 78
Ogumefun, 77
Ogundijo, Mathew, 18
Ohen, 23
Ohen Okun, 23
oil, 114
Oil Rivers, 3
Oil Rivers Protectorate, 4
Ojukwu, Colonel Odumegwu, 8
Okrika, 2
Okonkwo, Dr. C.E., 12, 15, 20, 131
oligarchy, 115
Olu, 26, 131
Olunloyo, 31
Oluwole, 32
Olu's princes, 26
on peasant farms, 128
Ondo, 40, 75, 78
Ondo Boys' High School, 79
One major Nigerian Language, 145
One Nigerian Language, 145
One of Physics, Chemistry and Biology, 146
onion, 30
Onitsha, 116
Onitsha, a Boy's Boarding School, 73

Onitsha Town, 74
Open Sesame, 67
opinions, 11
opportunities, 122
opposition, 61
Oral history, 16
oral poetry, 17
ordeal, 14
Ordinances, 54, 87, 93, 94
ordinary school, 73
ordinary primary school, 46
organizations, 94
Orlu, 96
Oron Training Institute, 79
Ossai, King Obi, 67
Owen, Captain, 37
Owerri, 78
Owerri Province, 96
Oxford, 42
Oyo, 32, 75, 78

Pacification, 4
pagans, 58, 82, 83, 118
pain, 102
painters, 38
Palmer, H.R., 43
Papal decree, 23
parastatals, 109
Parent-Teacher Associations, 119
parental homes, 19
Parents, 16, 17, 119, 125
Paris, 39
Parliament, 29
participation, 16
Partitioned, 3
Pathfinders, 98
Pathfinders of European Imperialism, 82
people, 12, 122, 129
Persuasion, 3
Pastors, 38
Pategi, 42, 43
Pax Britannica, 54

payment by results, 87
pen-pushers, 77
per capita levels, 108
periodic reports, 85
periodical examinations, 87
permanent, 144
personnel, 96
Phillips, Edward, 30, 31
Phillipses, 77
Phillipson Grants-in-Aid of Education, 88
Philosophy, 16, 143
Philosophy of education, 115
Philosophy of Nigerian Education, 143
physical activities, 16
physical and biological sciences, 114
physical and intellectual skills, 146
Physical education, 125, 145, 146
physical self, 16
physical training, 13
physical violence, 102
physical well-being, 15, 16
physique, 16
piazza, 20
Pires, Duarte, 24
plaiting, 19
planning, 117
plant, 16, 19
Plateau, 92
play, 16, 17
Plough, 29, 30
poetic chants, 17
poetic verses, 16
poetry, 13, 21
policy initiatives, 128
policy program, 119
political, 23, 82, 120, 128
political and religious leaders, 83
political and social significance, 58
political and spiritual leaders, 8
political arena, 71
political instrument, 93

political invasion, 98
political leaders, 71
political leadership, 71
political movement, 98
political participation, 13
political patronage, 108
political power, 26
political problems, 129
political reasons, 54
political revolution, 95
political scene, 111
political socialization, 101
political stability, 115
political, social and economic tool, 101
Political system, 1
Political units, 7
Political wishes, 3
politics, 29, 68, 128
Polytechnic Courses, 147
Polytechnics, 128, 146
poor, 38
poor communication network, 45
poor country, 100
poor planning, 89
poor soil, 18
poorly educated, 85
poorly organized, 22
population, 127
Population Reference Bureau, 126
Portugal, 2, 23-26
Portuguese merchant, 23, 25
Portuguese Missionaries, 24
Portuguese monarch, 23
porous soil, 18
position of marginality, 102
post-school certificate, 114
post-secondary education, 114, 146
post-secondary institution, 106
poverty, 63
power, 101
practical agriculture, 145
practical farming, 13

practical men, 93
praises, 16
pre-colonial Nigeria, 11
pre-colonial times, 11
preaching tours, 21
precepts, 21
pre-primary, 143
Pre-Primary Education, 143
Presbyterian, 37, 38
Presbyterian Church, 36
Presbyterian Church of Scotland, 28
Presbyterian Mission, 86
Presbyterians, 64
presents, 24
prestige, 70
Pre-Vocational Subjects, 145
preparation for a broad-based education, 144
preparation for useful living, 144
prevocational, 144
priests, 17,19, 24, 103
prima facie, 12
primary, 87, 120, 143
primary and secondary grammar schools, 77
primary and secondary levels, 117
primary and secondary schools, 121
primary and secondary school education, 95
primary education, 120, 125
primary school, 47, 52, 81, 87, 89, 91, 105, 106,
primary school classrooms, 120
primary school curriculum, 57
primary school education, 108, 118, 143, 144
primary school enrollment, 89, 127
primary school level, 108
primary school population, 108
primary schools in Nigeria, 126
primitive communities, 95
Prime Ministers, 128
Prince, 25, 27

Princes' Middle School, 53
private car, 116
private control, 102
private enterprise, 101
private sector, 109
privileges, 102
production factor, 115
productivity, 29
professionals, 17
professionals in law, 77
professions, 17, 19, 114
profits, 29
profitable investment, 115
programs, 96
progress, 100
Progress and Certification, 144
proliferation of schools, 103
promiscuity, 56
Propaganda Fide, 77
Propagation of the Faith, 40
prophecy, 19
propriety control, 117
proselytization, xix, 59, 62, 70
protective, 13, 15, 16
Protectorate of Northern Nigeria, 4, 5
Protectorate of Southern Nigeria, 5
Protestant, xviii, 64, 71, 73, 75, 76
Protestant and Catholic Missionaries, 61
Protestant Awakening, 28
Protestant Institution, 71
Protestant Missions, 71
Protestant Missionaries, xviii
Protestant Missionary societies, 28
Protestant Schools, 118
Protestant teachers, 71
proverbs, 13, 15, 16
Provincial headquarters, 47, 52
Provincial schools, 48
provision of health, 108
psychological, 124
psychological fabric, 88
public and private sectors, 88

public concern, 93
public life, 15
public schools, 48
publishing houses, 122
punitive measures, 4
pupils, 39, 53, 77, 81
purdah, 104

qualification, 22, 116
quality of education, 118
Quran, 20-22, 83, 84
Quranic school teachers, 22
Queens, 19
Queen of England, 33
Queen's ship, 37
quota system, 106, 107
quota system alone, 107
quota system of admission, 107
Quranic schools, 43, 47

Racing, 13, 16
rainmakers, 19
rank, 101
rational decisions, 124
raw materials, 29
rearing, 16
reasoning, 13, 16
recitation, 13, 16, 17
recognize, 18
Recreational subjects, 13
re-election, 8
Regional Houses of Assembly, 88
regions, 1, 91, 112
relate to education, 125
relatives, 17, 18
Religion, 1, 20, 26, 44, 69, 91, 103, 112
Religious, 23, 41, 63, 75, 82, 86
Religious affiliation, 99
Religious cleavages, 118
Religious conflicts, 92
Religious Instruction, 144
Religious invasion, 98

Religious lines, 118
Religious men, 50
Religious organizations, xix, 62
Religious practices, 47
Religious reformers, 21
Religious studies, 145
Religious tensions, 118
repetition, 17
Report on the Review of Education in Eastern Nigeria, 96, 97
representatives, 88
Republic of Biafra, 8
Resident, 7, 42, 51, 58
Resident Major, 6, 43
respect, 12, 102
respectable, 12
responsibilities, 59, 117
retentive memory, 17
revenues, 108
rhymes, 17
riddles, 13, 16
right type of values, 143
right type of values and attitudes, 123
Rio del Rey, 3
rite, 14
rituals, 13, 19
rivalries, 97
rivalries between missions, 96
rivalry, 61, 94, 96, 97
River Benue, 3
River Niger, 39
River Volta, 39
rivers, 19
Robertson, Sir James, 28
Roman Catholic, 74
Roman Catholic children, 71
Roman Catholic curriculum, 72
Roman Catholic favor, 69
Roman Catholic High School, 73
Roman Catholic Holy Ghost Fathers, 42, 74, 80
Roman Catholic influence, 70

Roman Catholic Mission, 64, 65, 69, 72, 96
Roman Catholic Missionaries, 61
Roman Catholic Missionary, xvii, 39, 41, 63
Roman Catholic Policy, 118
Roman Catholic priests, 24
Roman Catholic Schools, 66, 72, 73
Roman Catholics, 39, 62, 71-73, 99, 118
Romans, 22
Romanists, 73, 74
royal charter, 3
Royal Niger Company, 2, 3, 4
Ruler of Warri, 131
rulers, 19, 36, 57
ruling class, 102
ruling elites, 118
running of the schools, 117
rural areas, 129
rural and urban areas, 95, 122
Ryder, A.F.C., 26

sanctity of marriage, 13
sacrament, 27
salaries, 116, 117
Salary Review Commission, 117
salary scale, 116
salvation, 33
sales representatives, 81
Salisbury Square, 67
Samaila, 53
Samaila, the Emir of Argungu, 52
sanitation, 87
Sankore, 21
Santo Agostinho, 27
Sao Thome, 24, 26
Sarauta, 7
Sardauna of Sokoto, 109
savings, 116
Savior, 34, 68, 71
scales of salaries, 116
scholars, 87

Schon, Rev. J.F., 68
school, 20, 21, 27, 30, 34, 36, 40, 47, 50, 51, 53, 55, 56, 62-65, 67, 70, 72, 75, 77, 82-85, 87, 88, 92, 93, 95-97, 99, 103, 105, 115, 117, 118, 119, 120, 122, 127
school-age children, 132
School committees, 119
School curriculum, 92
School of Agriculture, 146
School of Forestry, 146
School Revolution, 62, 64
School Revolution in Nigeria, 69
School-age Population, 76
Schoolmasters, 85
Schools and Colleges, 128
science, 96
scientific age, 22
scientists, 35
scions, 59
Scotland, xviii, 36, 61
Scottish Free Church Mission, 38
scramble, 62
scramble for Africa, 2
Seafaring, 18
Seasons, 16
Sebastian, 26
secede, 8
secondary, 143
Secondary and Teacher Training Institution, 77
Secondary classes, 116
Secondary education, 105, 145
Secondary grammar schools, 105
Secondary modern schools, 106
Secondary school, 39, 70, 71, 73, 75, 77, 81, 95, 106
Second-class Citizen, 13
Second National Development Plan, 121, 122
Secondary, 120
Secondary school, 124

Secondary school education, 124, 126
Secondary school enrollment, 126
Secondary school program, 124
secret cults, 16
secret societies, 14
secular education, 27, 73
secularized the ownership of schools, 120
selection of text books, 91
self-development, 123, 125
self-governing, 4
self-help, 119
self-learning, 125
self-government, 104
self-reliant identity, 101
Semi-Bantu, 2
Senior, 143
Senior Certificate, 116
Senior School Certificate, 143, 146
Senior secondary school, 124, 145
Separation, 13
sermons, 118
servants, 30
servants of the Emirs, 47
Sexual intercourse, 19
Shagari, Alhaji Shehu, 8
Shaikh, Uthman dan Fodio, 84
shame, 14
Shanahan, Bishop, xvii, 63
Shanahan, Father, 63, 64, 6-71
sharp, 99
Sharp, Granville, 28, 42
shelter, 22
sincere, 99
shipwrecked, 42
shoes, 48
Shonekan, Ernest, 8
Shorthand, 146
shrubs, 19
Sierra Leone, 30, 32, 33, 35, 87
Sierra Leone ex-slaves, 30
Simeon of Igboho, 35

Simple Sciences, 46
Sister Colette, 40
Sister Veronique, 40
skilled, 11, 12
slave trade, 27, 29, 37
slaves, 37, 67
Slessor, Mary, 38
Sobo, 2
Sociability, 15
social, 95
Social and Economic Development, 101
social change, 71, 100
social circumstances, 123
social control, 93, 102
social development, 115
social direction, 101
social problems, 95
social order, 12
social psychology, 16
social responsibility, 13
social sciences, 114,
social scale, 67
Social Studies, 144, 145
social values, 13
socially relevant, 101
Société des Missions Africaines, 75
society, 12, 146
society at large, 64
Society for African Missions, 28, 39, 40
Society of the Holy Ghost Fathers, 67
socio-economic groups, 123
sociological, 120
Sodeke, 34, 40
soil, 18
Sokoto, 5, 6, 43, 48, 56, 57, 105
Sokoto Emirate, 57
Sokoto Province, 53, 56
Sokoto Provincial School, 48
Sokoto State, 120
soldiers, xix

175

solidarity, 15
Son of God, 55
sons, 24, 50, 52, 53
sons of Chiefs and Emirs, 46, 47
sons of commoners (talakawas), 53
sons of native rulers, 94
sorcery, 27
soul, 19
South, 1, 5, 41, 42, 50, 57, 58, 81, 103, 104, 106-108, 111, 120, 121, 127, 131
South America, 36
Southern, 109
Southern applicants, 110
Southern Baptist Convention, 63
Southern Baptist Mission of America, 42
Southern domination, 112
Southern governments, 104
Southern Nigeria, xix, 4, 62, 64, 66, 70, 72, 77, 80, 81, 84, 85, 87-89, 103, 107, 115
Southern Nigeria Administration, 85
Southern Nigerians, 67, 81
Southern parts of the country, 107
Southern Provinces, 88
Southern religions, 107, 110,
Southern States, 89, 106
Southerners, 45, 108, 109, 111, 112
sovereignty, 66
spade, 45
Spanish Capuchin Missionaries, 25
specialization, 19, 146
specialized as follows, 128
spiritual and moral values, 13
spiritual values, 124
spoken art, 17
St. Andrew's College, 79
St. Charles' Training College, 70, 79
St. Gregory's College, 40, 70, 79
St. Mary's Convent school, 40
St. Matthew, 68
St. Paul's Training College, 79

St. Thomas' College, 79
states, 8
staff, 45
staffing arrangements, 117
standard, 94, 96, 118
State, 92, 106, 118
State colleges of education, 128
State Control of Education, 98
State Governments, 97-99, 113, 117, 118
State Governments in Nigeria, 115
States of the Federation, 127
status, 22
status cleavages, 102
storm, 18
story-relays, 13
story-telling, 13
straightforward, 32
strikes, 116
strong and self-reliant nation, 122
structure, 124
student enrollment, 106
student enrollment trends, 121
Student Teachers, 85
students, 82, 119, 126
study of Nigerian languages, 128
subjugation of Zinder, 58
Sudan, 35, 36
Sudan Interior Mission, 43
Sudan Party, 42
Sudan United Mission, 42
sugar, 40
Sule, the Emir of Fika, 57
Sultan Abubakar's generation, 52
Sultan of Sokoto, 44, 51, 55
Sultan of Sokoto Hassan, 56
Sunday schools, 31
Superior of Holy Trinity Mission, 69
supervisors, 88
survival of the individual, 123
swamp rice, 30
swift, 99
swimming, 16

sympathy, 94
Syria, 50

Tafsir, 21
tailors, 38
Take-over of mission schools, 99
Take-over of schools, 92, 126
Talakawa's sons, 53
Taylor, P.A., 67, 81
Taylor, Rev. J.C., 62
Teacher, 19-21, 24, 30-32, 38, 47, 49
Teacher education pogram, 91
Teacher-evangelists, 86
Teacher Training, 145
Teacher Training College, 70, 120
Teacher Training Institution, 31, 77, 86
Teachers, 70, 77, 81, 85, 95, 116, 120
Teachers and Headmasters, 144
Teachers Colleges, 145
Teachers in Government schools, 116
Teaching force, 120
Teaching Qualifications, 116
Teaching Staff, 87
technical, 47
technical and professional education, 100
technical and vocational training, 124
Technical Colleges, 145
Technical Colleges of education, 128
Technical Drawing, 146
Technical education, 96
Technical, industrial and agricultural education, 47
technical teachers, 116
technocrats, 36, 77
technological civilization, 114
technology, 96
Temple, 7
Ten years, 99

Tenets of Islam, 83
Tenets of the religion, 21
ten-mile piece of land, 39
territories, 83,96, 97
tertiary institutions, 128
The Joint Bishops' Circular on Education, 99
theological differences, xviii, 61
Things Fall Apart, 15
Third National Development Plan, 122
Thomas, Rev. W. Risk, 38
Tibenderana, P.K., 50-52, 54, 55, 57
tide and ebb, 18
Timbuctu, 21
Tiv, 1, 2
togetherness, 12, 13
tokenism, 59
tone, 87
Topo, 39, 40
topography, 16
Toronto Industrial Mission Missionaries, 42,
tortoise, 15
Toundi, 14
Townsend, Rev., 30, 34, 35
trade, 23, 68
traders, xix, 19, 62, 98
trading, 17, 18
trading posts, 2
tradition, 7, 50
traditional, 11, 131
traditional African dances, 16
traditional African education, 15
traditional circumcision ceremony, 14
traditional curriculum, 20
traditional education, 11-13, 16, 20
traditional groove, 95
traditional institutions, 6
traditional Nigerian society, 14
traditional rivalries, 96
traditional society, 11, 14-17

traditionalists, 118
Traditions, 11, 13
Traditions of Islamic Society, 82
trained and skilled manpower, 120
training, 19, 85
Training College, 74
training facilities, 125, 128
Training Institution, 31, 54, 70, 107
training of the mind, 143
transmit, 11
transport facilities, 108
trekking, 52
tribal rite, 14
tributary Kingdom of Benin, 131
tropical diseases, 30
truth, 82
Tuggar, Abubakar, 112
turbulence-free, 54
Tugwell, Bishop, 74
Turkey, 50
Turner, Captain, 36
Twi, 2
two world wars, 7
type of school, 99
Typewriting, 146

Ubah, C.N., 55, 59
Uchendu, Victor, 101, 128
Ugandans, xviii, 61
Ughoton, 23
Ulama, 22, 83
Umar Ibu Muhammed Al Amin Al Kenemi, the Shebu of Bornu, 52
uncompromising, 99
Undergraduates, 77
understanding of the world, 123, 143
unequal distribution of educational facilities, 122
unequal in the world, 129
unequal stratification system, 129
uniform standards, 119
unitary state, 112
united, 122

United Missionary College, 79
United Nations Declaration, 100
United Nations General Assembly, 100
United States, 115
United States of America, 115
united, strong and self-reliant nation, 123
unity, 12
Universal basic education, 125
Universal Declaration of Human Rights, 100
Universal free primary education, 119, 120
Universal free primary education scheme, 119
Universal free secondary education, 180
Universal Primary Education, 91, 104, 127
Universal Primary Education Programs, 89
Universal Primary Education Schemes, 88, 109
Universalist Religion, 82
Universities in Nigeria, 126, 128
Universities of Science and Technology, 128
University, 108, 126, 146, 147
University degree, 109
University graduates, 116
University of Ibadan, 107
UPE, 127
UPE program, 120
Upper Benue, 5
urban and rural areas, 105
urban and rural districts, 122
urban centers, 129
USA, 42
useful citizens, 95
Usman, 56
Usman Nagogo, the Emir of Katsina, 52

Usman, the Emir of Gwandu, 56
USSR, 115
utensils, 19

vacuum, 113
valedictory, 32
values, 20
vegetable gardens, 30
Venn, Henry, 29, 30, 131
verbal art, 17
vernacular, 47, 72
vertical, 105
vestibule, 27
Vicar Apostolic, 30
Vicariate of the Bight of Benin, 39
Vice Chancellors of Universities, 128
Vice President, 29
Victorian Englishmen, 28
Victorians, 29
village, 96
Village Heads, 19
Village School, 70, 95
Village School Phase, 69
virtues, 20
Vischer, Dr. Hans, 46, 50
vocation, 20, 21
vocational education, 17
vocational subject, 146
voluntary agencies, 93, 98
voluntary agency schools, 116

Waddell, Rev. Hope, 37-39, 63, 86
Walker, F. Deaville, 34
war, 24
Waratu, 33
wards, 53
Warri, 26, 27, 78
Waterside, 74
Wauters, Father, xvii, 103
Waziri, 58
wealth, 101
wealth of the countries, 115

weapons, 24
weavers, 47
weaving, 13, 17-19
Wesley, John, 28
Wesleyan agent, 42
Wesleyan Methodist, 34, 75
Wesleyan Methodist Committee, 35
Wesleyan Methodist Mission, 62
Wesleyan Methodist Missionary Society (WMMS), 28
Wesleyan Missionary, 33
Wesleyan Missionary Society, 42
Wesleyan Training Institute, 79
Wesleyans, 35
West, 1, 32, 75, 76, 89, 90, 91, 106
West Africa, 98, 105, 106, 108, 113, 114, 117
West African Company, 2
West African Examination Council, 146
West African lands, 4
West African spheres, 4
West African Territories, 87
West and East Regional Governments, 89
West Indian teachers, 43
West of Nigeria, 75
West of the Niger, 65, 66, 76
Western bank, 3
Western cultural values, 97
Western education, 23, 34, 41, 44, 46, 49-53, 83, 103, 104, 131
Western Equatorial Africa, 75
Western Governments, 109
Western Lines, 83
Western Nigeria, 2, 75, 89
Western education, xix
Western Region, 8, 132
Western Regional Government, 89
Western State Budget, 89
Western-educated Sierra Leone Immigrants, 77
White Fathers, xviii, 61

Whites to colonize blacks, 102
Whitaker, C.S., 7
white man, 37, 66, 68
white man's education, 59
white man's letters, 67
white missionaries, 57
white power, 67, 81
widows, 38
wife, 13
Wilberforce, William, 28
Wilhelm, Andrew, 30
Willoughby, Mr., 30
Witchcraft phlegm, 19
wives, 31
women, 19, 83, 102
women in Nigerian universities, 128
women teachers, 127
wood carving, 19
Woodwork, 146
workers, xvii
workshops, 19
World, 6
worship, 21
wrestling, 13
writing, 68
Wusasa, 58
Wushishi, 43

Xavier, 36

Yaba, 116
Yahaya, the Emir of Gwandu, 52
Yakubu, the Emir of Bauchi, 52
Yaqub, the Emir of Bauchi, 84
yeoman services, 117
Yola, 5
Yoruba, 1, 2, 17, 36, 77, 112, 113, 126
Yoruba Country, 77
Yoruba Towns, 77
Yoruba wars, 77
Yoruba hunters, 17
Yoruba Kingdom of Oyo, 2

Yoruba language, 36
Yoruba notes, 55
Yoruba women, 56
Yorubaland, xvii, 3, 4, 20, 32, 36, 39, 40, 75, 131
Yorubas, 76, 77
youth, 16

Zambezi, 115
Zaria, 5, 43, 48, 58, 108
Zaria City, 42, 58

STUDIES IN THE HISTORY OF MISSIONS

1. Daniel M. Davies, **The Life and Thought of Henry Gerhard Appenzeller (1858-1902): Missionary to Korea**
2. Johnathan J. Bonk, **The Theory and Practice of Missionary Identification (1860-1920)**
3. Samuel J. Rogal, **John Wesley's Mission to Scotland 1751-1790**
4. James L. Cox, **The Impact of Christian Missions on Indigenous Cultures: The "Real People" and the Unreal Gospel**
5. Gwinyai H. Muzorewa, **An African Theology of Mission**
6. J.R. Oldfield, **Alexander Crummell (1819-1898) and The Creation of An African-American Church in Liberia**
7. Stewart D. Gill, **The Reverend William Proudfoot and the United Secession Mission in Canada**
8. Harvey J. Sindima, **The Legacy of Scottish Missionaries in Malawi**
9. Samuel J. Rogal, **John Wesley in Ireland, 1747-1789**
10. Alan G. Padgett (ed.), **The Mission of the Church in Methodist Perspective: The World is My Parish**
11. Samuel J. Rogal, **John Wesley in Wales, 1739-1790: Lions and Lambs**
12. Karl-Wilhelm Westmeier, **The Evacuation of Shekomeko and the Early Moravian Missions to Native North Americas**
13. Martin E. Lehmann, **A Biographical Study of Ingwer Ludwig Nommensen, 1834-1918: Pioneer Missionary to the Bataks of Sumatra**
14. Fray Gerónimo de Mendieta, *Historia Eclesiástica Indiana*: **A Franciscan's View of the Conquest of Mexico**, critically reviewed, with selected passages translated from the original by Felix Jay
15. Magnus O. Bassey, **Missionary Rivalry and Educational Expansion in Nigeria, 1885-1945**